Tax Policy Reforms 2025

OECD AND SELECTED PARTNER ECONOMIES

OECD
BETTER POLICIES FOR BETTER LIVES

This work was approved and declassified by the Committee on Fiscal Affairs on 13/08/2025.

This document, as well as any data and map included herein, are without prejudice to the status of or sovereignty over any territory, to the delimitation of international frontiers and boundaries and to the name of any territory, city or area.

The statistical data for Israel are supplied by and under the responsibility of the relevant Israeli authorities. The use of such data by the OECD is without prejudice to the status of the Golan Heights, East Jerusalem and Israeli settlements in the West Bank under the terms of international law.

Note by the Republic of Türkiye
The information in this document with reference to "Cyprus" relates to the southern part of the Island. There is no single authority representing both Turkish and Greek Cypriot people on the Island. Türkiye recognises the Turkish Republic of Northern Cyprus (TRNC). Until a lasting and equitable solution is found within the context of the United Nations, Türkiye shall preserve its position concerning the "Cyprus issue".

Note by all the European Union Member States of the OECD and the European Union
The Republic of Cyprus is recognised by all members of the United Nations with the exception of Türkiye. The information in this document relates to the area under the effective control of the Government of the Republic of Cyprus.

Please cite this publication as:
OECD (2025), *Tax Policy Reforms 2025: OECD and Selected Partner Economies*, OECD Publishing, Paris, https://doi.org/10.1787/de648d27-en.

ISBN 978-92-64-54056-9 (print)
ISBN 978-92-64-68411-9 (PDF)
ISBN 978-92-64-32113-7 (HTML)

Tax Policy Reforms
ISSN 2617-3425 (print)
ISSN 2617-3433 (online)

Foreword

This report was produced by the Tax Policy and Statistics Division of the OECD's Centre for Tax Policy and Administration. It was led by Daniel Fichmann under the supervision of Bert Brys, and written jointly by Daniel Fichmann, Stéphane Buydens, Felix Estgen, Patrice Ollivaud (Economics Department), Ruairi Sugrue, and Astrid Tricaud. The authors would like to thank the delegates of Working Party No.2 on Tax Policy Analysis and Tax Statistics in its Inclusive Framework format and the OECD/G20 Inclusive Framework on Base Erosion and Profit Shifting (BEPS) for their inputs, as well as colleagues Piet Battiau, Assia Elgouacem, Pierce O'Reilly, Sarah Perret, and Kurt Van Dender for their contributions and comments. The authors would also like thank Karena Garnier for her assistance with editing and Michael Sharratt for his support with data processing.

The report was approved by the OECD/G20 Inclusive Framework on BEPS on 13 August 2025 and prepared for publication by the OECD Secretariat.

Table of contents

FIGURES

TABLES

Executive Summary

***Tax Policy Reforms: OECD and Selected Partner Economies* is an annual publication that provides comparative information on tax reforms across countries**. It tracks tax policy developments over time and describes the latest tax reform trends. This year's edition focuses on tax reforms introduced or announced during the 2024 calendar year in 86 jurisdictions.

With 2023 marking a turning point away from the broad tax relief measures seen during the pandemic and the subsequent period of inflation, this trend solidified in 2024 with a mix of rate increases and targeted tax support across all major tax types. High levels of debt coupled with significant emerging spending needs relating to climate change, ageing and, in some countries, increased defence spending, has meant that jurisdictions of all income levels have adopted strategies to mobilise more revenues. Some have opted to raise standard value added tax (VAT), corporate income tax (CIT), or personal income tax (PIT) rates, as well as health and environmentally related taxes. Others have pursued more targeted approaches to increase tax revenues, including the introduction of temporary or permanent excess profit taxes or surtaxes. These measures vary in scope, with some countries levying them on specific sectors, highly profitable firms, or directly on excess profits themselves.

In 2024, PIT and social security contribution (SSC) reforms increasingly reflected a balance between revenue-raising objectives and targeted support measures. More jurisdictions raised top PIT and capital income tax rates than in previous years, often to generate revenue or enhance tax progressivity. While base narrowing measures continue to be used to alleviate cost-of-living pressures, support measures in 2024 became more targeted and less reliant on broad relief compared to the response during the energy price crisis. Countries also expanded relief for young workers, families, and the elderly. Meanwhile, SSC rate increases remained widespread amid rising health and ageing-related spending, while SSC base reforms were more balanced. Base broadening measures focused on increasing maximum contribution thresholds and expanding the range of covered income, whereas SSC base narrowing measures targeted specific types of workers or sectors to stimulate labour force participation.

Signs that the downward trend in CIT rates has halted or is reversing grew stronger in 2024, with more jurisdictions increasing rates than reducing them for the second consecutive year. While many governments continued to prioritise support for investment, there was a notable pivot towards revenue mobilisation, particularly through rate increases. Nonetheless, base narrowing measures were common, as governments continued to offer tax incentives for investments, particularly in research and development, clean technologies, and strategic sectors.

While the use of reduced VAT rates as a policy instrument remained widespread in 2024, their role continued to shift from crisis management towards more targeted objectives. Many jurisdictions expanded or extended VAT relief on essential goods and services – such as food, energy, health, housing, and childcare – primarily with the stated objective of addressing equity and cost-of-living concerns. However, as inflationary pressures eased, a number of countries began scaling back temporary VAT cuts introduced during the pandemic and subsequent energy price crisis. At the same time, revenue mobilisation objectives prompted several countries to raise their standard VAT rate. Finally, health excise tax reforms continued to gain momentum as a tool to both mobilise revenue and support public health goals, with many jurisdictions increasing taxes on tobacco, alcohol, and sugar-sweetened beverages.

Another notable shift in 2024 is the move away from temporary fuel tax reliefs towards increases in fuel excise taxes. In 2022 and 2023, many countries reduced excise taxes on fossil fuels used in road transport and electricity to ease cost-of-living pressures. From 2024, however, countries have started to increase fuel excise tax rates again. At the same time, high-income countries also continued to strengthen explicit carbon pricing for the second consecutive year, with several increasing carbon tax rates or expanding their scope to include new sectors, such as international shipping and agriculture.

Additionally, the use of tax policy to support the transition to a low-carbon economy continued to broaden. Governments combined carbon pricing with targeted tax incentives, including reduced VAT rates for goods and services linked to environmental sustainability, PIT relief for sustainable transport, and CIT incentives for clean investments. These behavioural incentives to promote low-carbon consumption and investment, are increasingly embedded across all major tax types. By contrast, tax policies aimed at encouraging healthier lifestyles rely primarily on excise taxes. Nonetheless, health related excise tax reforms continued to gain momentum in 2024, as many jurisdictions raised taxes on tobacco, alcohol, and sugar-sweetened beverages to support public health objectives and increase revenues.

Property tax reforms predominantly focused on rate cuts and base narrowing measures. Most measures sought to ease the tax burden on households, make housing more affordable, simplify property tax systems, and encourage investment. Where property tax increases did occur, they were primarily driven by the need to raise revenue and address equity or fairness concerns.

1 Macroeconomic background

This chapter provides background information on macroeconomic conditions until the end of 2024. Tax revenues and reforms are closely linked to macroeconomic conditions, including variations in economic growth, inflation, productivity, investment, the labour market, and public debt. This chapter gives a brief overview of recent trends in these areas to put the tax policy reforms discussed in chapter 3 in context.

Global GDP is estimated to have grown by 3.3% in 2024, around 0.2 percentage points below the 2010s average (Figure 1.1), strengthening to 3.7% in the last quarter (seasonally adjusted, annualised rate) (OECD, 2025[1]). Robust real income gains and lower interest rates generally supported household spending growth. However, this was offset in some regions by weaker government spending, partly related to the withdrawal of fiscal support measures that were introduced in response to the energy crisis, and by sluggish consumer confidence – despite strong household income growth – weighed down by the continuing impact of past high food and energy inflation (Ollivaud and Westmore, 2024[2])

Among advanced economies, GDP growth remained robust in the United States, Denmark, Greece, and Spain. In contrast, growth was weaker elsewhere, with real GDP per capita estimated to have declined in nearly one-third of OECD countries in 2024. Some countries, notably in Europe, saw a significant slowdown of GDP growth in 2024 compared to the average over 2010-19. These included Austria, Estonia, Hungary, Iceland, Israel, Latvia and New Zealand. In Japan, annual growth was also sluggish, though there were signs of an upturn towards the end of the year. The second half of the year was also relatively buoyant for Canada, Chile, Denmark, Israel and the Netherlands.

Figure 1.1. Average annual real GDP growth

In percent

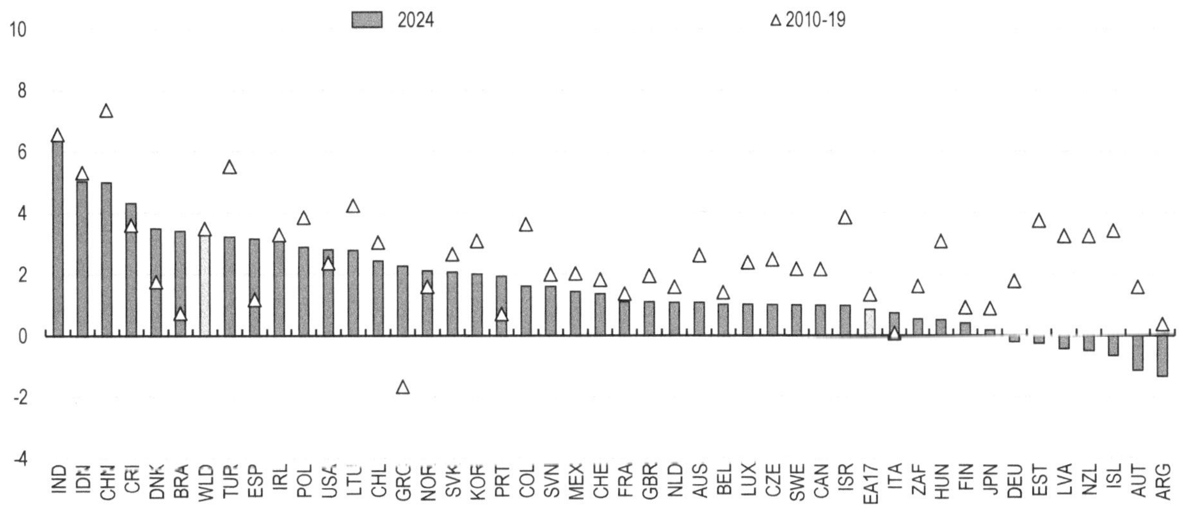

Note: Aggregates are calculated using weights in purchasing power parities except the euro area (EA17), for which countries are weighted by GDP in euros. Growth in India is based on fiscal years starting in April. Growth in Ireland was computed using gross value added at constant prices excluding foreign-owned multinational enterprise dominated sectors. The data in this figure are based on the OECD Economic Outlook and therefore do not cover all of the jurisdictions included in this Tax Policy Reforms report.
Source: OECD Economic Outlook 117 database; and OECD calculations.

StatLink https://stat.link/yf9ce3

Emerging-market economies exhibited diverse growth patterns. India, Indonesia and China recorded the strongest GDP growth rates among reported countries in 2024 (Figure 1.1). The pace of growth in Colombia and the Republic of Türkiye was weaker than the average during the previous decade, while growth in Brazil was stronger. Meanwhile, the fourth quarter of 2024 was particularly strong in many countries. While rapid growth in Brazil slowed, the pace of economic activity remained robust in India, South Africa and Türkiye, and the recession in Argentina continued to abate. GDP growth in China remained solid in the second half of 2024, with private consumption supported by government incentives and rapid export growth.

Global trade growth rebounded in 2024 but eased slightly in the final quarter of the year. Trade patterns during 2024, particularly between Asia and North America, were affected by the need to manage risks related to shipping availability at peak times and by longer journey times due to the effective closure of the Red Sea route and lower water levels in the Panama Canal. Services trade remained relatively buoyant through 2024, helped by a continued recovery in international travel and tourism.

Headline and core inflation in the OECD and major emerging-market economies peaked in the second part of 2022 and have declined since (Figure 1.2). Amongst emerging-market economies, inflation rates in Argentina and Türkiye increased to high levels during 2024 but began to fall later in the year. The evolution of inflation rates through 2024 was generally characterised by decreasing goods inflation, while services inflation proved more resilient. However, median of goods inflation rate across OECD countries started to rise in the last few months of 2024 (from -0.3% in September to 1.5% in December, year-on-year) while services inflation remained elevated, raising concerns about the extent to which inflation would further moderate.

Figure 1.2. Inflation rate since 2015

Year-on-year, in percent

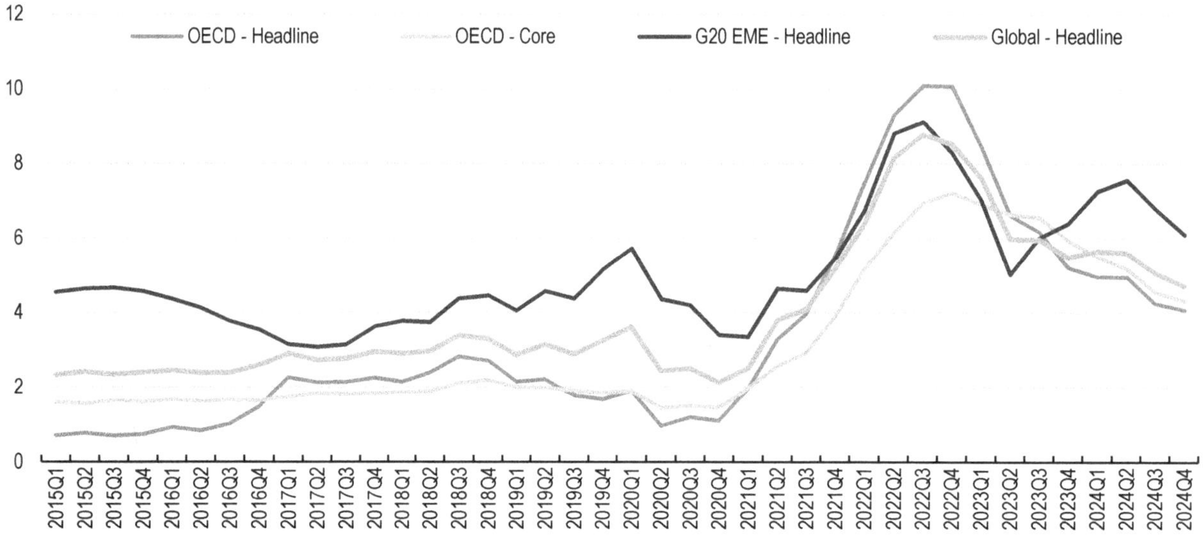

Note: Core is a measure of inflation excluding food and energy products. The data in this figure are based on the OECD Economic Outlook and therefore do not cover all of the jurisdictions included in this Tax Policy Reforms report.
Source: OECD Economic Outlook 117 database; and OECD calculations.

StatLink https://stat.link/cxs3ov

Labour market conditions remained generally favourable, although employment growth slowed somewhat in the second half of 2024. Unemployment remained low in most countries, with the OECD-wide unemployment rate at 4.9% at the end of 2024, below the pre-pandemic level of 5.3% (Figure 1.3). The largest decreases from pre-pandemic levels were for Costa Rica, Greece, Italy, Spain and Türkiye. In contrast, some increases in unemployment rates were recorded for Canada, Denmark, Estonia, Finland, Hungary and Sweden. Nominal wage growth continued to ease through the second half of 2024 alongside lower price inflation, but remained elevated, with wage pressures lingering in some regions. In most advanced economies, strong wage growth, accompanied by relatively modest productivity gains, kept unit labour cost growth above levels consistent with central bank inflation targets.

Policy interest rates began to decline in most major economies during 2024. Notable exceptions included Japan and Brazil, where policy interest rates were increased. The monetary policy stance at the end of the year remained restrictive in most countries, with forward-looking real interest rates above pre-pandemic norms and policy interest rates generally above estimates of long-term equilibrium levels. Borrowing costs eased through the year for many firms and households in OECD economies, but the effect of past increases in policy rates continued to be felt as rates on existing loans were renegotiated and new higher-yielding debt was issued. Overall, indicators suggested that financial conditions eased materially in 2024 in both advanced and emerging-market economies.

Housing investment is estimated to have fallen by about 4% in the median OECD economy in 2024, partly in response to relatively high interest rates. In China, the correction in the real estate market continued, with housing investment declining. However, some signs of a pick-up in housing market activity materialised in some countries, with the number of transactions beginning to recover in France, Korea, Spain and the United Kingdom. In addition, real business investment remained generally weak amid tight financing conditions and sluggish demand in some economies. Nearly half of OECD countries with available data reported a contraction in business investment in 2024, including Canada, France and Germany.

Figure 1.3. Unemployment rates in OECD countries

As a percentage of the labour force

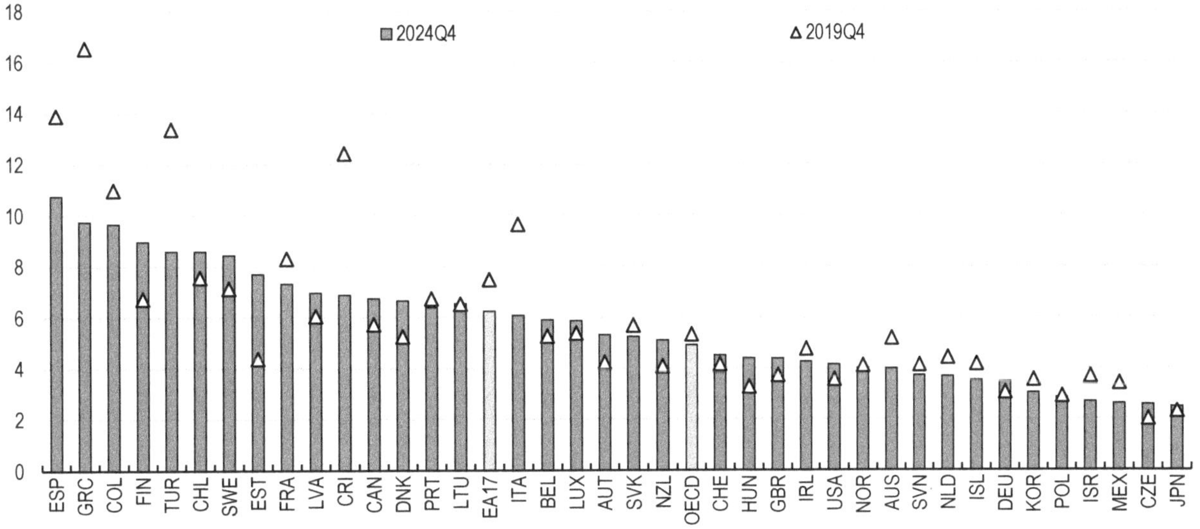

Note: 2024Q3 for Iceland. The data in this figure are based on the OECD Economic Outlook and therefore do not cover all of the jurisdictions included in this Tax Policy Reforms report.
Source: OECD Economic Outlook 117 database; and OECD calculations.

StatLink https://stat.link/2bdwg4

As a percentage of GDP, public debt in 2024 was higher than before the pandemic for most countries (Figure 1.4). For the OECD as a whole, government debt rose by around 8 percentage points, reaching nearly 112% of GDP in 2024. Debt service costs have risen substantially since 2021 partly reflecting higher interest rates now compared to when maturing debt was issued. Headline fiscal deficits as a share of GDP increased in 2024 for about half of OECD countries. There were a few exceptions, with the deficit shrinking in Czechia, Estonia, Hungary and Italy. After adjusting for the economic cycle, and removing net debt interest payments, there was little fiscal consolidation in most OECD economies in 2024.

Figure 1.4. General government gross debt

As a percentage of GDP, 2024

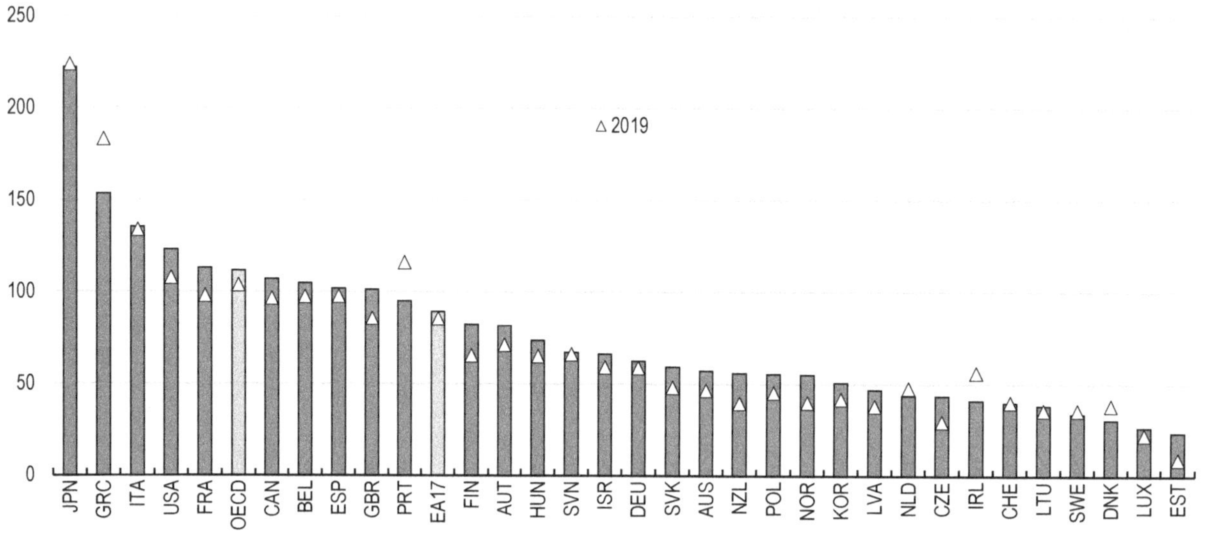

Note: Maastricht definition for EU countries. The data in this figure are based on the OECD Economic Outlook and therefore do not cover all of the jurisdictions included in this Tax Policy Reforms report.
Source: OECD Economic Outlook 117 database

Macroeconomic conditions have played a key role in shaping recent tax policy reforms. While the causal relationship between macroeconomic dynamics and specific tax policy decisions remains underexplored, several patterns have emerged. Rising public debt levels have emerged as a motivation for revenue-raising reforms, particularly in light of mounting fiscal pressures (Romer and Romer, 2010[3]). High inflation has also influenced tax policy, putting pressure on household budgets – especially where wages have been slow to adjust – prompting governments to provide relief through both targeted and broad-based measures.

References

OECD (2025), *OECD Economic Outlook, Interim Report March 2025: Steering through Uncertainty*, OECD Publishing, Paris, https://doi.org/10.1787/89af4857-en. [1]

Ollivaud, P. and B. Westmore (2024), “The key role of food and energy inflation in shaping consumer confidence”, *OECD Ecoscope blog*, https://oecdecoscope.blog/2024/12/13/the-key-role-of-food-and-energy-inflation-in-shaping-consumer-confidence/. [2]

Romer, C. and D. Romer (2010), “The Macroeconomic Effects of Tax Changes: Estimates Based on a New Measure of Fiscal Shocks”, *American Economic Review*, Vol. 100/3, https://doi.org/10.1257/aer.100.3.763. [3]

2 Tax revenue context

This chapter is based on the OECD Global Revenue Statistics Database and its accompanying publications. It describes the latest tax revenue trends, analysing both total tax-to-GDP ratios and tax structures over time, across low-, middle-, and high-income countries, focusing on OECD countries in particular.

This chapter presents the latest trends in tax revenues, analysing both overall tax-to-GDP ratios and the composition of tax revenues across all 38 OECD countries, as well as low-, middle-, and high-income countries covered by the OECD Global Revenue Statistics database. It highlights developments in tax-to-GDP ratios and tax structures, with a particular focus on patterns observed over the past two to three years. Due to the limited availability of 2023 data, the primary emphasis of the analysis in this chapter is on OECD countries, though averages for non-OECD high-, middle-, and low-income economies are also included. Preliminary data for 2023 is available for 36 OECD countries, while for other jurisdictions, or income groups, the most recent data pertains to the year 2022.

In 2023, the average tax-to-GDP ratio across OECD countries declined by 0.1 percentage points to 33.9%. Among the 36 countries with available preliminary data for 2023, the ratio rose in 18, fell in 17, and remained unchanged in one. Revenues from taxes on goods and services, as a percentage of GDP, declined in 22 countries, with an average drop of 0.5 percentage points. Property tax revenues also fell in 27 OECD countries. By contrast, revenues from Social Security Contributions (SSCs) increased in 24 countries.

For jurisdictions where 2022 is the most recent year with available data, the tax-to-GDP ratio increased in all regions that are covered. In Africa, the average tax-to-GDP ratio across 33 countries rose by 0.5 percentage points, reaching 16% of GDP in 2022. In the Latin America and Caribbean (LAC) region, comprising 27 countries, the ratio increased by 0.3 percentage points to 21.5%, while the Asia-Pacific region, covering 36 economies, recorded an increase of 0.6 percentage points to 19.3%. From an income group perspective, high-income countries (HICs) experienced a slight decrease in their average tax-to-GDP ratio, down 0.1 percentage points to 31.6% in 2022. In contrast, the ratio rose by 0.7 percentage points to 18.9% in middle-income countries (MICs), and by 0.3 percentage points to 13.5% in low-income countries (LICs).

The overall composition of tax revenues remained broadly stable in 2022 relative to 2021 across income groups (OECD, 2024[1]). The tax mix in OECD countries was largely similar to the patterns seen over the past decade. Between 2021 and 2022, the combined share of personal and corporate income taxes in total tax revenues rose by 1.4 percentage points to reach 36.5%. Within this increase, the share of corporate income tax (CIT) grew, while the share of personal income tax (PIT) declined. Meanwhile, the average share of SSCs fell by 0.8 percentage points, and the share of revenues from taxes on goods and services declined by 0.4 percentage points. These trends were mirrored across different income groups, where only minor or no shifts in the tax mix were observed. On average, HICs rely more heavily on PIT compared to MICs and LICs. In contrast, MICs and LICs continue to derive a significantly larger share – over half – of their tax revenues from taxes on goods and services.

2.1. Trends in tax revenue levels

Tax revenues continue to differ widely across countries. However, there is a long-term trend of convergence in tax-to-GDP ratios, as LICs and MICs have steadily increased their tax revenues over the past three decades (Figure 2.1). Among OECD countries, differences in tax-to-GDP ratios have also continued to narrow gradually, with countries at the lower and upper end of the distribution moving closer to the OECD average.

Between 2019 and 2022, tax-to-GDP ratios in high-, middle-, and low-income countries remained relatively stable, despite the severe economic disruptions caused by the COVID-19 pandemic. Part of this stability reflects the fact that both GDP and tax revenues declined during the crisis; since tax-to-GDP is measured relative to GDP, a fall in both can leave the ratio broadly unchanged. As economies began to recover, tax revenues rebounded along with economic activity. Regionally, the Asia-Pacific average returned to its pre-pandemic level by 2022. African countries continued efforts to strengthen their fiscal systems, contributing to gradually rising tax-to-GDP ratios over the past decade. In LAC the tax revenue gains were more modest than in 2021. This was largely due to a challenging macroeconomic environment marked by slowing growth and rising inflation. While high prices and output in the oil and mineral sectors supported increased revenue from non-renewable resources, these were partially offset by lower revenues from consumption taxes, reflecting government efforts to cushion inflationary pressures on households and businesses.

In 2023, nominal tax revenues rose in 31 of the 36 OECD countries for which data is available, while nominal GDP increased in 33. In 12 cases, the tax-to-GDP ratio declined as tax revenues grew more slowly than GDP. In Chile, Korea, Israel, and the United States, the ratio also declined, but due to a nominal drop in tax revenues despite GDP growth (OECD, 2024[1]). Meanwhile Norway saw a decline in both indicators, with tax revenues falling more sharply than GDP. On the other hand, 18 countries recorded an increase in their tax-to-GDP ratios compared to 2022. In 16 of these, tax revenues outpaced GDP growth. In Ireland and Denmark, the rise in the ratio was driven by falling nominal GDP alongside an increase in tax revenues.

Figure 2.1. Tax-to-GDP ratios since 1990

Tax revenues as a percentage of GDP

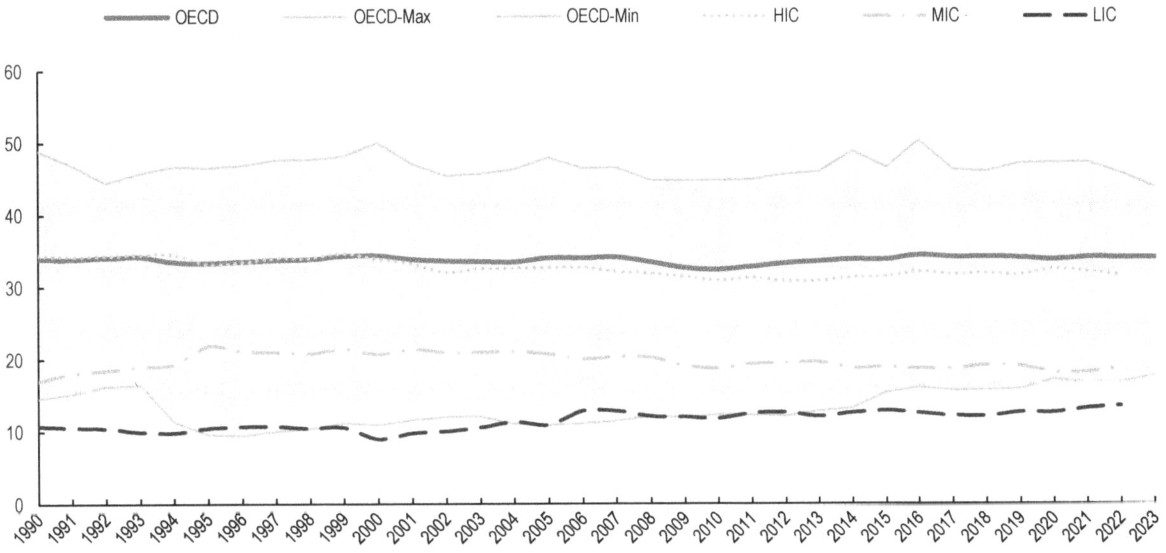

Note: The maximum and minimum OECD values signal the range. See the Global Revenues Statistics database for more information.
Source: Global Revenue Statistics Database.

StatLink https://stat.link/gu2p0v

2.2. Trends in tax structures

As with the level of tax revenue, the composition of tax structures varied considerably across OECD countries in 2022. Eighteen countries derived the largest share of their tax revenues from income taxes – encompassing both PIT and CIT – while eleven countries relied primarily on SSCs. In nine countries, consumption taxes, including VAT, were the dominant source of revenue. In contrast, property and payroll taxes accounted for a relatively small portion of tax collections across most OECD countries in 2022 (Figure 2.2). In LICs and MICs, consumption taxes tended to represent the largest share of total tax revenues, placing them more firmly within the latter group.

Changes in tax-to-GDP ratios across countries in 2022 reflected a relatively even distribution between increases and decreases, though with a slight overall bias toward increases. Among the 17 countries where the tax-to-GDP ratio declined, Chile experienced the most pronounced drop – 3.3 percentage points – largely driven by a reduction in income tax revenues (Figure 2.3). Korea, Israel, and the United States also recorded notable declines, each exceeding 2 percentage points. On the other hand, Luxembourg posted the largest increase in its tax-to-GDP ratio, rising by 2.7 percentage points, primarily due to higher revenues from PIT and SSCs. Colombia followed closely with a 2.5 percentage point increase, attributed to stronger CIT revenues. Türkiye also recorded an increase of more than 2 percentage points. Additionally, the large decline in CIT revenues in Norway between 2022 and 2023 primarily reflects the exceptional profits of the energy industry in 2022.

Figure 2.2. Tax structures in 2022 (as a % of total tax revenues)

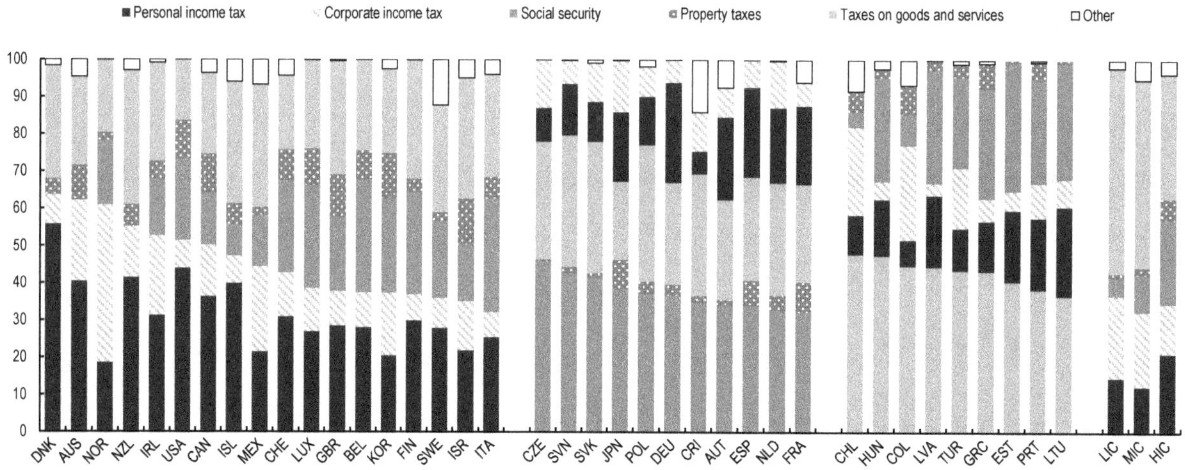

Note: Countries are grouped and ranked by those where income tax revenues (personal and corporate) form the highest share of total tax revenues, followed by those where social security contributions, or taxes on goods and services, form the highest share.
Source: Global Revenue Statistics Database.

StatLink https://stat.link/n73ikc

Figure 2.3. Decomposition of change in OECD tax-to-GDP ratios by tax type, 2022-23

Year-on-year change, p.p.

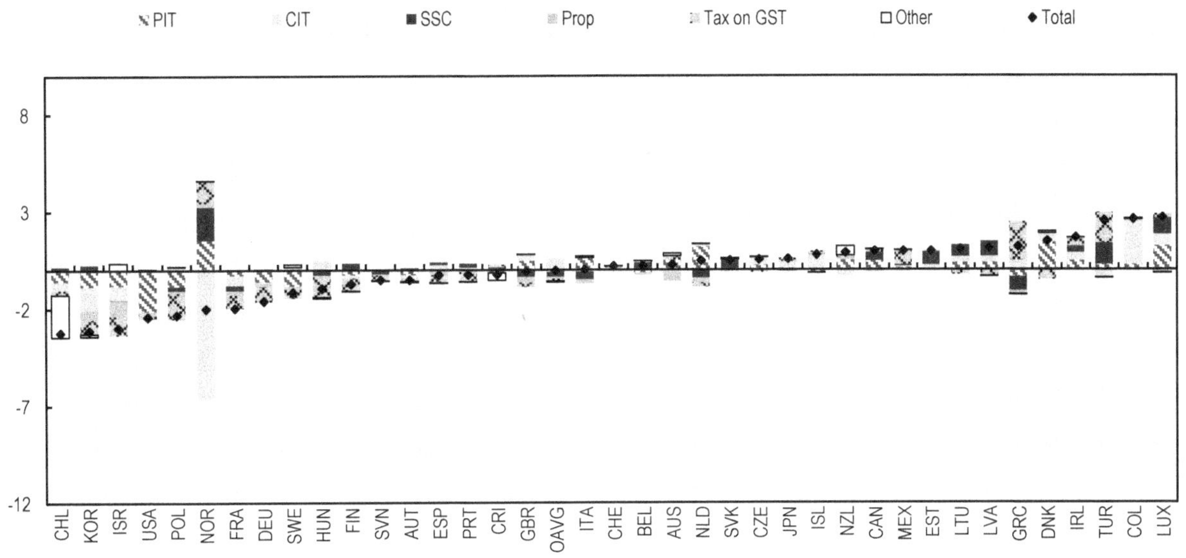

Note: Data for 2023 are preliminary and should be interpreted with caution. This graph includes the change between years 2021 and 2022 for Australia, Greece, Japan, Poland and the OECD average. Disaggregated data for 2023 for these countries were not available at the time of publication.
Source: OECD Revenue Statistics (2024).

StatLink https://stat.link/8r127h

Reference

OECD (2024), *Revenue Statistics 2024: Health Taxes in OECD Countries*, OECD Publishing, Paris, https://doi.org/10.1787/c87a3da5-en. [1]

3 Tax policy reforms

This chapter provides an overview of the tax reforms adopted by 86 member jurisdictions of the OECD/G20 Inclusive Framework on Base Erosion and Profit Shifting that responded to the OECD's annual tax policy reform questionnaire, including all OECD countries. It reviews the reforms that were announced and implemented between 1 January 2024 and 31 December 2024, examining trends in each category of tax, including personal income taxes and social security contributions, corporate income taxes and other corporate taxes, consumption taxes, environmentally related taxes, and taxes on property.

3.1. Introduction

The analysis in this chapter is primarily based on countries' responses to the 2025 annual Tax Policy Reform Questionnaire, which was completed by 86[1] member jurisdictions of the OECD/G20 Inclusive Framework on Base Erosion and Profit Shifting at the start of 2025. The annual questionnaire described in Box 3.1 asks responding jurisdictions to describe their tax reforms as well as to provide details on their expected revenue effects and other relevant information, including the rationale for the tax measures. The following sub-section empirically summarises tax reforms in high-income countries from 2015 to 2024. The sections that follow focus on tax reforms introduced or announced between 1 January 2024 and 31 December 2024 and examine trends in each category of tax including personal income taxes and social security contributions (Section 3.2), corporate income taxes and other corporate taxes (Section 3.3), taxes on goods and services, including VAT/GST, sales taxes and excise duties (Section 3.4), environmentally related taxes (Section 3.5) and property taxes (Section 3.6).

Box 3.1. The OECD Annual Tax Policy Reform Questionnaire

At the Working Party No.2 on Tax Policy Analysis and Tax Statistics (WP2) meeting in November 2009, delegates from OECD countries agreed to start systematically collecting information on the main tax measures adopted in each country. The motivation for this proposal was to provide consistent and comparative information on tax reforms to inform policy discussions in OECD and non-OECD countries. At the November 2010 WP2 meeting, the following criteria were agreed for deciding whether a tax policy measure was sufficiently substantial to be reported in the questionnaire:

- A significant change in a total tax rate;
- A change in the tax base that is expected to change revenue from that base by more than 5% of total tax revenue or 0.1% of GDP; and
- A politically important systemic reform.

Any central or sub-central tax policy measure that was implemented, legislated, or announced in the previous calendar year that meets at least one of the criteria listed above must be reported in the questionnaire.

For each reform, the questionnaire requests information on the type of tax; the dates of entry into force, legislation, or announcement; the direction of the rate and/or base change; and a detailed description of the reform. The questionnaire also asks for the rationale behind the reform and estimates of the revenue effects of the tax measures.

3.1.1. Empirical trends in tax reforms over the last decade (2015 – 2024)

The data suggest that the trend toward tax decreases observed during the COVID-19 pandemic and subsequent inflation has slowed and, in some cases, began to reverse. Figure 3.1 below shows the weighted direction of tax reforms in high-income countries between 2015 and 2024. Each reform included in the figure is assigned a weight between 0 and 1, based on the absolute size of its projected annual revenue impact, following the methodology described in Box 3.2. This weighting is applied at the level of individual tax reforms, allowing the figure to reflect the relative significance of each reform across countries, years, and tax types. The larger the projected revenue impact of a reform, the higher its weight (up to a maximum of 1). The indicator shown in Figure 3.1 represents the net direction of reforms, calculated as the average difference between the sum of weighted tax-increasing and tax-decreasing reforms. Importantly, it should not be interpreted as the average projected revenue impact itself, but rather as a measure capturing the direction and intensity of reforms over time.

PIT and SSCs reforms continue to show divergent trends. On average, the number and magnitude of PIT-decreasing reforms has outweighed those increasing PIT over the past decade. The average reform direction indicator in Figure 3.1, however, suggests that this gap closed significantly in 2023 before widening again slightly in 2024. This change reflects that although high-income countries have continued to implement reforms lowering the PIT burden on households, both the number of high-income countries doing so and the scale of the reforms were smaller than during and prior to the pandemic. In contrast, SSC reform trends in high-income countries have shifted more decisively. After consistent reductions between 2015 and 2021, the average direction of SSC reforms turned to increasing in 2022 and markedly so in 2023, before easing somewhat in 2024. The trend towards more increases also reflects the mounting fiscal pressures linked to ageing populations and growing demands for social protection.

Figure 3.1. Average reform direction of tax reforms implemented in high-income countries over the 2015 – 2024 period

Average reform direction indicator (described in Box 3.2 below)

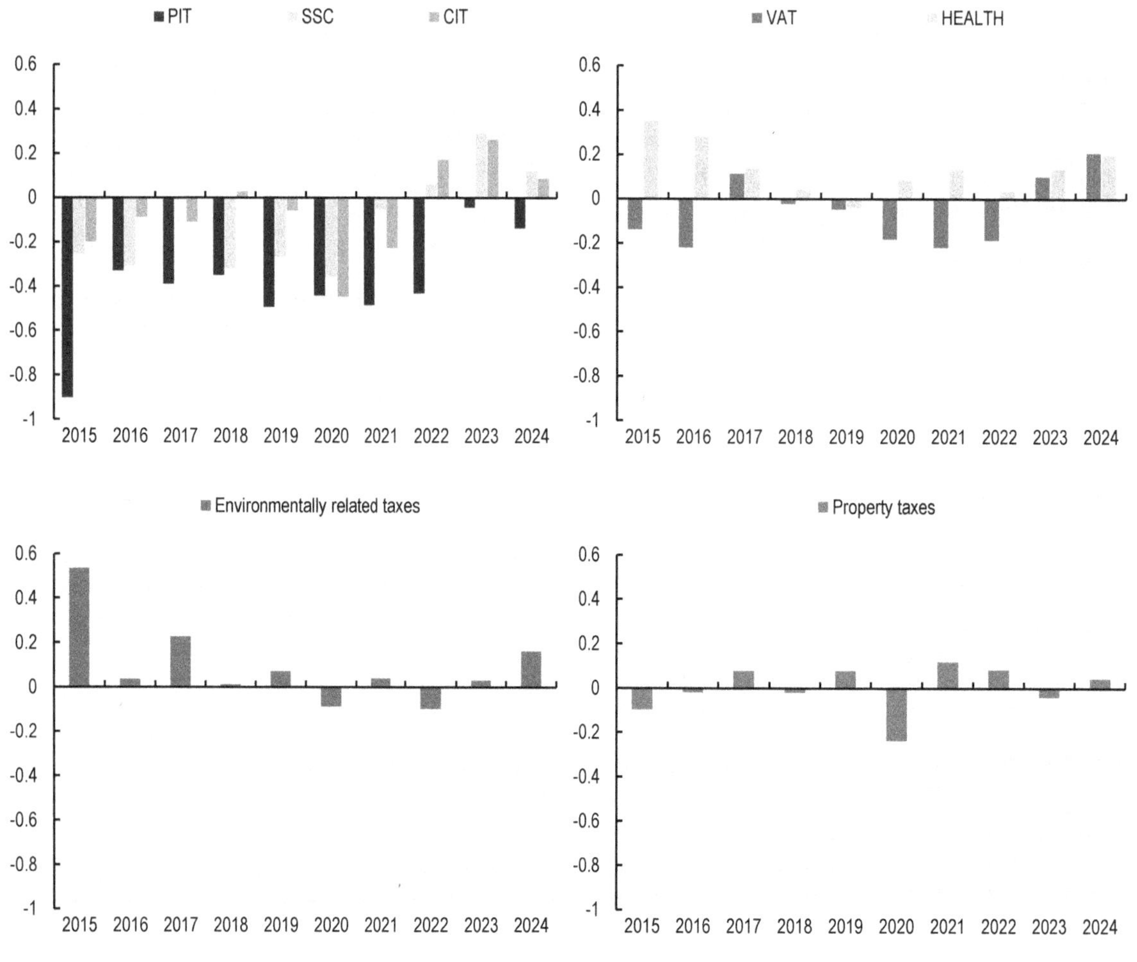

Note: The values in this figure are calculated using only the reforms for which revenue impact data was made available
Source: OECD Annual Tax Policy Reform Questionnaire and author's calculations.

StatLink https://stat.link/3tn1g8

The trend of CIT rate reductions showed further signs of halting in 2024, as the average direction of CIT reforms appeared to have shifted away from tax reductions since 2022. While the period up to and including the pandemic were dominated by CIT reducing reforms, Figure 3.1 indicates that high-income countries have implemented more revenue-increasing reforms from 2022 onward.

While most countries introduced VAT reductions during the pandemic and subsequent period of energy price pressures, 2023 appeared to mark a turning point, followed by further VAT-increasing reforms in 2024. This shows that the rollback of pandemic-era relief measures and temporary consumption tax cuts introduced during the cost-of-living crisis has continued in 2024. It also reflects the significant efforts to increase tax revenues by some countries, which raised their standard VAT rate. Similarly, countries have also increased their focus on increasing health related excise taxes in 2024 and 2024.

The direction of environmentally related tax reforms has varied significantly in recent years. In 2022 and 2023, many countries temporarily reduced fuel excise taxes in response to surging energy prices and broader inflationary pressures. The 2023 cuts are not visible in Figure 3.1, since a handful of countries increased their carbon taxes, leaving the average reform direction close to neutral. In 2024, however, the rollback of temporary fuel and energy tax reductions, along with the introduction of fuel and carbon tax increases, marked a clear change in direction. Finally, the direction of property tax reforms remained mixed throughout the period, with no sustained trend.

Box 3.2. Calculating the reform direction using tax revenue impact information

Let $R_{j,i,t+p}$ denote the nominal revenue impact for reform j in country i in period $t+p$ (using the revenue information provided in the questionnaire for up to 4 years).

1. The average reported revenue impact over P_j years is calculated as:

$$\overline{R_{j,i,t}} = \frac{1}{P_j}\left(\sum_{p=1}^{P_j} R_{j,i,t+p}\right)$$

2. The average revenue is divided by $GDP_{i,t}$ to standardise:

$$r_{j,i,t} = \frac{\overline{R_{j,i,t}}}{GDP_{i,t}}$$

3. The standardised values are winsorised at the 2.5 and 97.5 percentile. A common practice with noisy data that involves replacing the extreme high and low values of $r_{j,i,t}$ with the nearest values within those thresholds to ensure that outliers do not skew the results.

4. The absolute value of the standardised revenue impact is normalised using the min-max approach in order to obtain a weight that ranges from 0 to 1:

$$weight_{j,i,t} = \frac{|r_{j,i,t}| - min(|r_{j,i,t}|)}{max(|r_{j,i,t}|) - min(|r_{j,i,t}|)}$$

   Where $|r_{j,i,t}|$ is the absolute value of the standardised revenue impact for a reform j, in country i, and year t; and $min(|r_{j,i,t}|)$ and $max(|r_{j,i,t}|)$ are the global minimum and maximum values of $|r_{j,i,t}|$ computed over the entire dataset of available reforms (including all countries and years). This approach ensures that the normalisation is performed relative to the extreme values found in the entire dataset, providing a consistent scale for all data points.

   We normalise the data in order to re-scale the value for the weight between 0 and 1, allowing us to count the reforms as in previous years while also taking their significance into account. Thus, the revenue data is only used as a proxy for the significance of a reform, as we do not want the indicator to be falsely interpreted as a revenue forecast.

5. Once the weight is calculated, reforms are categorised into tax increasing, tax decreasing and neutral reforms and grouped into CIT, PIT, SSC, VAT, environmentally related tax (ENV), and health related tax (HEALTH) reforms. We then sum the weights of all tax increasing measures and the weights of all tax decreasing measures in each country i, for each tax type x, and year t and calculate the difference. Meaning that at the end we are left with a $Direction_{i,x,t}$ measure for country i, tax type x, and year t:

$$Direction_{i,x,t} = \sum_{j}^{J_{i,x,t}} \left(weight_{j,i,x,t} * I(increase_{j,i,x,t})\right) - \sum_{j}^{J_{i,x,t}} \left(weight_{j,i,x,t} * I(decrease_{j,i,x,t})\right)$$

   Where $J_{i,x,t}$ is the total number of reforms in country i for tax type x and year t; $weight_{j,i,x,t}$ is the normalised weight associated with reform j for country i tax type x and year t; and lastly $I(increase_{j,i,x,t})$ is an indicator function assigning the value 1 if the reform j is a tax increase and 0 otherwise.

6. To obtain the values in Figure 3.1 we calculate the annual average of the difference across countries for CIT, PIT, SSC, VAT, environmentally related taxes (ENV), and health related taxes (HEALTH):

$$AverageReformDirection_{x,t} = \frac{1}{N_{x,t}}\left[\sum_{n}^{N_{x,t}} Direction_{i,x,t}\right]$$

Where $N_{x,t}$ is the number of high-income countries in the dataset for tax type x and year t. $Direction_{i,x,t}$ is the country specific difference of the sum of weighted tax increases and the sum of weighted tax decreases for each country i tax type x and year t.

The resulting indicator, $AverageReformDirection_{x,t}$, is presented in Figure 3.1. and shows the average direction of tax reforms across high-income countries for each tax type and year from 2015 to 2023.

3.2. Personal income tax and social security contributions

Cost-of-living concerns continued to drive a significant share of PIT reforms in 2024. In response to the persisting impact of rising general price levels and higher interest rates, many countries introduced PIT reforms to support low- and middle-income households, primarily in the form of base narrowing measures. Compared to previous years, reforms tended to be more targeted and discretionary inflation adjustments were less wide-ranging. At the same time, the 2023 pattern of removing or scaling back existing allowances and credits appears to have slowed down in 2024. Affordability was a key consideration for reforms to personal capital income taxation as well, with a number of reforms aiming to counteract elevated rents and housing prices.

Some countries also raised top PIT and capital income tax rates to generate more revenue. Overall, increases to top PIT rates were more common than in previous years and were mostly implemented as part of broader PIT reforms or with the goal of increasing tax revenues. Increases to taxes on capital income were typically aimed at enhancing the progressivity of the tax system. In general, the mix of PIT rate increases and decreases was more balanced than in 2023.

As in previous years, countries implemented a wide range of PIT reforms to support labour market participation and address demographic shifts. Several countries introduced or expanded tax relief for young workers, families with children, and the elderly. Others made use of targeted provisions to support employment in specific sectors or reduce the tax burden on employer-provided benefits. Additionally, a number of countries also expanded or introduced preferential tax regimes to attract high-skilled foreign workers.

Additionally, countries also sought to promote environmental goals through preferential PIT treatment of sustainable transport and housing investments. Reforms included tax exemptions or reductions for the private use of electric company cars, the provision of charging infrastructure, and the use of bicycles and other low-emission transport modes supplied by employers.

Against the backdrop of rising healthcare costs and population ageing, the number of jurisdictions implementing SSC rate increases remained elevated. While most changes to SSC rates were increases, base reforms were more balanced. Base broadening measures focused on increasing maximum contribution thresholds and expanding the range of covered income. Narrowing measures targeted specific types of workers or sectors, frequently with the aim of increasing formal labour force participation.

3.2.1. PIT and SSCs remain central in high-income countries but play a smaller role in lower-income economies

PIT and SSC are a central source of tax revenue in most high-income countries (HICs), while they play a more limited role in low- and middle-income countries (LICs and MICs) (Figure 3.2). In 2022, PIT and SSCs together accounted for over 44% of total tax revenues in HICs, compared to just under 23% in MICs and 20% in LICs. In LICs, the share of PIT and SSCs in total tax revenue rose by over 6 percentage points since 2000, reflecting, in part, the gradual strengthening of personal tax systems in those countries. In contrast, MICs saw a 5.7 percentage point decline over the same period. In HICs, the combined PIT and SSC share declined slightly – down nearly 3.1 percentage points from 2000.

Wide cross-country variation persists in the share of PIT and SSCs in total tax revenue. In 2022, PIT made up less than 10% of total tax revenues in countries such as Costa Rica, Colombia, and Czechia, but exceeded 50% in Denmark, which does not collect a significant amount of SSCs. By contrast, SSCs accounted for over 40% of total revenues in countries like Slovakia, Slovenia, and Czechia. Overall, the combined share of PIT and SSCs remained below 20% of total revenues in Chile and Colombia, while exceeding 60% in Germany and the United States. In terms of changes over time, Türkiye saw a decline in the share of PIT and SSCs in total revenues, falling by nearly 12 percentage points since 2019 and over 5 points since 2000. Norway also experienced a notable drop of 16.5 percentage points compared to 2019, due to exceptional profits in the energy industry, which increased the relative share of CIT revenues. Sweden recorded a long-term decline as well, with the reliance on PIT and SSCs revenues falling by more than 12 percentage points since 2000, partly due to a changed mix between SSCs and payroll taxes. In contrast, countries such as Mexico, Korea, and Costa Rica have significantly increased their reliance on PIT and SSCs since 2000.

Figure 3.2. Revenues from personal income tax and social security contributions, 2000, 2019 and 2022

PIT & SSC revenues as a percentage of total tax revenues

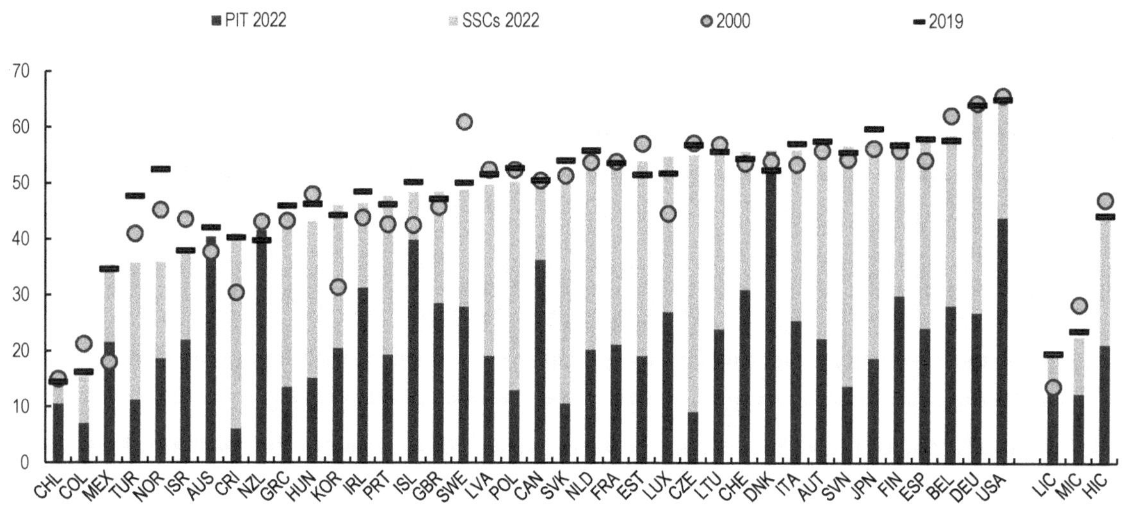

Note: Personal income tax revenues refer to tax category 1100 under the OECD classification of taxes, and social security contributions to tax category 2000. Tax revenues are the sum of taxes collected by all levels of government. See Revenue Statistics Interpretative Guide for more detail. The low- (LIC), middle- (MIC), and high-income country (HIC) averages are representative of the 120 countries that provide tax revenue data to the OECD.
Source: OECD Global Revenue Statistics Database

StatLink https://stat.link/8c3fer

3.2.2. While PIT rate cuts still outnumbered PIT rate increases, the mix of reforms was more balanced than in previous years

Four jurisdictions (Estonia, Isle of Man, Latvia, Norway) increased top PIT rates. To finance rising expenditures on defence, Estonia implemented its previously announced flat PIT rate increase from 20% to 22% in the form of an additional 2% Security Tax applying to the same base as the standard rate. In the case of the Isle of Man, the higher of its two PIT rates was increased from 20% to 22% with the primary objective of raising revenue to finance increasing expenditures on health services. The reform was announced as a temporary measure until the eventual introduction of a separate National Health Levy. Norway raised the rates of its top three brackets by one tenth of a percentage point, however, when the bracket rate hike and the SSC rate change are considered together, the marginal tax rate for taxpayers remained unchanged in brackets three to five, while it was reduced in brackets one and two.

In Latvia, the government raised PIT rates as part of a broad PIT reform. The two lower PIT rates of 20% and 23% were consolidated into a single bracket, with income up to EUR 105 300 being taxed at a rate of 25.5%. The highest marginal PIT rate on income above EUR 105 300 was raised from 31% to 33%. Furthermore, Latvia introduced an additional rate of 3% on total taxable income over EUR 200 000. As discussed below, the base for this additional rate was broadened to include certain types of capital income that in the general case are still exempt.

Table 3.1. Changes to personal income tax rates

	Rate increase		Rate decrease	
	2023	2024 or later	2023	2024 or later
Top PIT rate	DNK[2], KEN, NOR[5]	CAN[3], EST, IMN[4], LVA[1], NOR[5]	CAN[3]	HRV
Non-top PIT rate	ALB[1], KEN, NLD, NOR[5]	LVA[1], NOR[5]	CAN[3], DNK, GIB, HRV, IRL, ITA, MUS, PRT, SWE	AUS, CAN[3], GGY[2], HRV, IRL, NLD

Note: 1 denotes a new tax, 2 denotes reform announcement, 3 denotes that tax reform was implemented at the sub-central level, 4 denotes a temporary reform, 5 In Norway the SSC rates were reduced with the equivalent rate meaning that the marginal tax rate remained the same for taxpayers in bracket three to five, while it decreased in bracket one and two.
Source: OECD Annual Tax Policy Reform Questionnaire.

In the face of higher costs of living, cuts to non-top PIT rates in high-income jurisdictions frequently focused on reducing the burden on low-income earners. Australia, for example, reduced the rates levied on the first and second tax brackets from 19% to 16% and from 32.5% to 30%, respectively. The Netherlands introduced a new lowest tax bracket at a rate of 35.82% for box 1 income (employment and homeownership) up to EUR 38 441. Meanwhile, the marginal rate in the second bracket up to EUR 76 817 increased to 37.48%. Guernsey announced the introduction of a lower 10% rate on income up to GBP 30 000, above which the 20% rate continues to apply. Ireland reduced the rate of its Universal Social Charge by a further percentage point to 3% on income between EUR 27 382 and EUR 70 044. Italy made the consolidation of its tax rates from four to three brackets permanent, combining the first two tax brackets and keeping the lower rate.

Croatia lowered PIT rates across the board. Following the passing of a significant PIT reform in 2023, Croatia lowered the upper limits of the ranges between which local governments may set PIT rates. For instance, a town with fewer than 30 000 inhabitants can now set a lower rate in the range of 15% to 21% (previously 15% to 22.4%) and a higher rate in the range of 25% to 31% (previously 25% to 33.6%). The threshold for the higher rate also increased from EUR 50 400 to EUR 60 000.

3.2.3. PIT bases were narrowed to support cost-of-living and employment objectives following a long-term trend

The trend of jurisdictions implementing PIT base narrowing measures continued in 2024. While the motivations behind such measures remain varied, the majority of reforms was aimed at counteracting cost-of-living increases, especially for lower income households, and at supporting employment. Compared to previous years, there was an increase in reforms to the taxation of employer-provided benefits as well as reforms targeted at providing relief for younger taxpayers.

Table 3.2. Changes to personal income tax bases

	Base broadening		Base narrowing	
	2023	2024 or later	2023	2024 or later
Personal allowances, credits, tax brackets	FIN, KEN, NOR, PRT, SWE	CAN[5], NLD, NOR	ALB, ARG, AUS, AUT[4], CAN[5], COK, DEU[4], DNK, ESP, EST[3], FIN, HRV, IRL, ITA, LCA, LUX[1], MAC, MUS, NLD, NOR, PNG, PRT[1], URY, ZAF	AUS, BLZ, CAN[5], DEU, FIN, HRV, IRL, JPN, LUX, LVA, MAC, MLT, MSR, NAM, NOR
Self-employed and unincorporated business	GRC, NLD, TUR	IRL, SVN	FIN, IDN, LVA, MAC[1], TUR	GRC, MAC, SVK
Employment and specific industries	AUS[3], FRA, IND, ROU	NLD, ROU	AUT, BEL, BGR, DEN, FIN, FRA, IRL, KEN, MYS[1], PER, TUR	ARM, CAN[5], DNK[3], GRC, IRL, LUX, NLD, PRT, SVN, TUR
Provisions targeted at low-income earners, EITCs		FIN	CAN, DNK[3], FIN, IRL, LTU, NLD	CAN[5], FIN, IRL, ITA, KOR, MEX, GRL, SWE[3]
Employer-provided benefits			ITA, SVN	DEU, FIN, HUN, IRL, ITA, KEN, KOR, LVA, SVK, SVN
Children and other dependents	DEU, EST, NOR, PNG		BGR, CAN, GRC, HRV, IRE, ISR, KOR, LTU, MYS, URY	CAN[5], DEU, HRV, HUN, IRL, JPN, KOR, LUX, MUS, SVK
Elderly & disabled	EST, SWE		LUX, LTU, HRV, MYS	CAN[5], HRV, IRL, MUS
Miscellaneous expenses, deductions, and credits	CZE, DNK, EST, FIN, TUR	SWE, FIN	AUT, DEU, DNK, ESP[1], FIN[1], IRL[1], LVA, LUX, MEX[1], NLD, PRT[1], SVK, SWE[1], TUR, URU, ZAF	AUT, CAN[5], DNK[3], IRL, KEN, LUX, LVA

Note: 1 includes a temporary tax measure, 2 denotes a new tax, 3 denotes reform announcement, 4 denotes reforms introduced in 2023, but covered in 2024 edition, 5 denotes that tax reform was implemented at the sub-central level.
Source: OECD Annual Tax Policy Reform Questionnaire.

Bracket adjustments and enhanced allowances and credits remained key tools in responding to higher price levels

Countries continued to raise tax thresholds, though changes were often concentrated on lower income brackets rather than the broad discretionary inflation adjustments seen during the energy price crisis in 2021-22. Malta, for instance announced a widening of tax brackets targeted at low- and middle-income taxpayers, with the threshold for the top marginal PIT rate remaining unchanged. Similarly, Germany upward-adjusted the thresholds for all but the top bracket, while also increasing the exemption limit for its solidarity surcharge. Australia raised the thresholds of its two upper tax brackets for the 37% and 45% marginal rates. Finland partially adjusted its central government earned income tax scale to the rise in the general earnings level. For the first time since 2013, Namibia revised its PIT brackets, such that the tax-free threshold doubled from NAD 50 000 to NAD 100 000. Luxembourg adjusted its tax brackets to general price increases via its automatic indexation mechanism. Ireland raised the band for the income tax standard rate by EUR 2 000 while also adjusting the applicable thresholds for the Universal Social Charge. In Canada, the province of Nova Scotia adjusted its tax brackets for inflation, while Alberta introduced a new indexation framework under which bracket thresholds, credits, and allowances are indexed by the lesser of 2% or the annual growth rate of the Consumer Price Index.

Fewer jurisdictions increased the generosity of their basic tax allowances compared to previous years. In 2024, Germany increased its basic personal allowance from EUR 10 908 to EUR 11 784 to account for the impact of inflation. Similarly, Croatia raised its basic allowance on employment income from EUR 560 to EUR 600. Montserrat heightened its allowance by XCD 3 000 to XCD 18 000. Finland also raised its basic personal allowance. Several Canadian provinces (Nova Scotia, Prince Edward Island, and Saskatchewan) adjusted their basic personal tax exemptions including to account for inflation.

Some countries raised their tax exemptions. Latvia introduced a fixed minimum tax exemption for all taxpayers which is set to gradually grow from EUR 510 to EUR 570 over the coming years. Meanwhile, Lithuania revised the formula for the tax-exempt amount such that for some taxpayers earning more than the minimum wage a larger share of income is exempted. Belize increased its tax-exempt threshold of income from BZD 20 000 to BZD 29 000. Australia raised the tax exemption thresholds on its Medicare levy for singles, families, and seniors and pensioners.

To ease financial pressures from the rising cost-of-living, countries also implemented various other base narrowing measures, including increases to tax deductions and targeted credits. Japan increased the basic tax deduction by JPY 100 000 to JPY 580 000 and introduced additional deductions depending on the taxpayer's income level, while also raising the minimum guaranteed amount of the deduction for employment income by JPY 100 000 to JPY 650 000. Greenland increased the personal tax deduction by 25% to DKK 60 000. Macau (China) increased the standard tax deduction of the professional tax for employees by 5 percentage points to 30% and raised the standard income exemption from MOP 95 000 to MOP 144 000. Kenya increased the tax-deductible contributions to registered pension funds, provident funds, and individual retirement funds by 50% to KES 360 000. Kenya also introduced new deductions on contributions to the Social Health Insurance Fund as well as the affordable housing levy in accordance with the Affordable Housing Act. Luxembourg increased the maximum monthly amount of the minimum wage tax credit to EUR 81. Additionally, Luxembourg introduced measures aimed at offsetting the carbon tax burden for lower-income taxpayers by raising the maximum amount of the progressive CO_2 tax credit.

Selected base broadening measures aimed at phasing out relief measures or improving targeting

Some jurisdictions introduced base broadening measures with the aim of rolling back previous PIT relief measures or improving their targeting. The Netherlands reduced the basic tax credit by EUR 335, while linking its phase-out to the level of the minimum wage. The Netherlands also slowed the planned increase the top PIT bracket threshold by EUR 557 compared to the previously announced annual EUR 1 000 increase (on top of the automatic indexation mechanism). Finland decreased the maximum amount of the tax credit for household expenses to EUR 1 600. Sweden announced a phase-out of the tax deduction on interest for unsecured loans. Additionally, Sweden announced an abolishment of the tax deduction for micro-production of renewable electricity, a decreased tax deduction rate on the installation of solar panels to 15% and a raised threshold above which commuting expenses are tax deductible. Romania eliminated its PIT exemption of RON 10 000 for those working in the IT, construction, agriculture, and food industry. In Canada, Manitoba announced a phase-out of its basic personal tax credit for income between CAN 200 000 and CAN 400 000. Lastly, the Canadian province of Québec raised the eligibility age of its tax credit for career extension from 60 to 65, while also increasing the exclusion threshold and maximum amount for eligible work income.

Several jurisdictions introduced PIT reforms to encourage employment and support specific industries

Several jurisdictions (including Finland, Greenland, Ireland, Korea, and Sweden) increased the generosity of earned income tax credits with the aim of supporting employment. Greenland raised the rate of its earned income tax credit from 3% to 17.5%, alongside a higher maximum payout. Sweden announced an increased earned income tax credit and elimination of the phase-out of the credit. Finland abolished its earned income tax deduction. As a compensatory measure, however, it increased its earned income tax credit by 6 percentage points to 18% for qualifying income as well as raising the maximum amount which is set to increase with the number of children. Korea raised the income threshold for earned income tax credit eligibility for dual-income households by KRW 6 million to KRW 44 million. Ireland increased its personal tax credit, employee tax credit, and earned income tax credit from EUR 1 875 to EUR 2 000. Meanwhile, Mexico implemented successive increases to the rate of its employment subsidy deduction from income taxation. Finally, Italy introduced an automatically granted tax credit not included in taxable income equal to 7.1% of annual income if the latter is lower than EUR 8 500, 5.3% up to EUR 15 000, and 4.8% up to EUR 20 000. Additionally, it introduced a non-refundable tax credit for employees earning income up to EUR 40 000, with a maximum deduction of EUR 1 000.

Countries also introduced favourable tax provisions on certain types of income or bonuses. Greece introduced a tax exemption on tips up to EUR 300 per month. Ireland expanded the small benefit tax exemption from two qualifying incentives to five, while raising the maximum amount to EUR 1 500. Portugal introduced a tax exemption on voluntary payouts in the form of productivity bonuses, performance bonuses, or profit-sharing of up to 6% of the employee's base salary. Luxembourg expanded its participation premium, under which profit-sharing payouts benefit from a 50% tax exemption, such that it can now comprise up to 30% of a worker's total remuneration. The Netherlands raised the scope of the first bracket work-related-cost scheme, under which employers can provide untaxed allowances to employees, from 1.92% to 2% of income below EUR 400 000.

A small number of countries used targeted PIT incentives to support specific sectors. As part of a set of reforms targeted at the domestic high-tech sector, Armenia introduced a reduced 10% income tax rate on wages related to scientific research and development. Greece introduced separate taxation at a flat rate of 22% on the remuneration of on-duty doctors. Germany extended the option for income smoothing in the agriculture and forestry sector. Until 2028, income from agriculture and forestry can be evenly distributed over a three-year period in order to mitigate the negative impact of profit fluctuations under a progressive income tax schedule due to climate change and generally fluctuating weather conditions.

Denmark and Slovenia introduced changes to the taxation of compensation provided in the form of company shares. Denmark announced changes to the taxation of employee-owned stock aimed at facilitating share-based compensation by SMEs. Slovenia changed the point where a tax liability arises on share-based compensation for employees of start-up companies from the moment shares were transferred to the employee to the moment where shares are disposed or employment is terminated.

Three countries (Chile, Greece, and Peru) introduced tax measures aimed at increasing compliance. To promote the formalisation of its economy, Peru established a temporary income tax regime that applies to previously undeclared income. Under this special regime, any undeclared net taxable income generated until 31 December 2022 is taxed at a rate of 10% upon its declaration, or at 7% if the income is repatriated. To be considered repatriated, the income must remain in Peru for a minimum period of 12 months. Joining the regime results in the annulment of any sanctions or past tax liabilities regarding the previously unreported assets. Public officials and income located in jurisdictions classified as high risk or non-cooperative by the Financial Action Task Force (FATC) are ineligible for the regime. Greece introduced deductions for taxpayers that pay their tax owed by the deadline for the first instalment. A deduction of 2% to 4% can be applied to the total tax amount and other certified debts depending on the date the tax return is filed. Chile introduced a temporary regularisation scheme allowing taxpayers to declare previously undeclared foreign assets and related income (see Box 3.3). The scheme included a flat tax rate of 12%, which is applied to the previously undeclared assets and income.

Several jurisdictions enhanced PIT relief for families and the elderly

Several jurisdictions provided PIT relief for families with children and dependents with disabilities. Hungary announced a stepwise doubling of its family allowance, which increases with the number of dependent children, as well as of its allowance for dependents with disabilities. Similarly, Croatia raised the value of its allowance for children, with larger adjustments for families with more dependent children, as well as its disability allowance. Korea increased the amounts of its child tax credit, which increases with the number of dependent children or grandchildren. Additionally, Korea introduced a temporary tax credit for couples that register their marriage before the end of 2026. Ireland raised the amounts of its single person child carer tax credit, the incapacitated child tax credit, the dependent relative tax credit, and the blind tax credit. Luxembourg increased the amounts of its tax credit for single parents with children, with the largest increases going to taxpayers with lower earnings. Luxembourg also raised the allowance for extraordinary expenses for children not living in the household. Japan announced the introduction of an income exemption for parents for dependents aged 19 to 22 to account the adjustment of working hours by part-time student workers. The Slovak Republic restricted the child tax credit to children up to the age of 18 (previously 25), while changing the formula used to calculate the maximum amount of the credit in a way that will lead to larger benefits for low-income earners. Germany adjusted the basic tax allowance for children to inflation. In Canada, the provinces of Nova Scotia, Prince Edward Island, and Saskatchewan raised their PIT exemptions for dependent children and dependents with disabilities. Mauritius introduced an income tax deduction of up to MUR 60 000 per year and child for parents with children in full-time fee-paying private schools.

Ireland, Mauritius, and several Canadian provinces provided additional PIT relief for the elderly. Ireland raised its home carer credit by EUR 150 to EUR 1 950, while Mauritius introduced an income tax deduction of up to MUR 30 000 per year for the employment of a caretaker for elderly parents or grandparents. A number of Canadian provinces (Nova Scotia, Prince Edward Island, and Saskatchewan) adjusted their personal tax exemptions for seniors for inflation.

PIT reforms for the self-employed remained limited

Greece made several significant revisions to its taxation of self-employed workers. It abolished the professionals' levy for the self-employed. It also adjusted the method of calculating the minimum imputed income of freelancers from comparison with the highest-paid employee's salary such that the taxable amount will be reduced in some cases. Lastly, Greece introduced a 50% reduction of the deemed income of self-employed individuals who are resident in municipalities with fewer than 1 500 inhabitants.

A few jurisdictions also reduced taxes on the self-employed. Macau (China) narrowed the base of its professional tax on the self-employed, raising the standard tax deduction from 25% to 30% and the standard income exemption from MOP 95 000 to MOP 144 000. Sweden announced improved tax conditions for sole proprietorships and traders as well as simplified rules on loss carry forward. The Slovak Republic raised the threshold below which self-employment income benefits from a lower 15% rate by EUR 40 000 to EUR 100 000. Albania reversed the previous year's reforms expanding the taxation of certain self-employed individuals due to a constitutional court decision.

A few European countries expanded taxation on self-employed workers or unincorporated businesses. Slovenia reduced the relevant maximum annual revenue thresholds for eligibility to its flat-rate regime for self-employment income by 40% to EUR 60 000 for fully insured persons and EUR 30 000 for individuals that are not fully insured. Ireland introduced an additional 3% surcharge on self-employment income above EUR 100 000 for its Universal Social Charge. Croatia established new rate ranges for the flat-rate income tax (per bed) on short term rentals through a flat-rate business, which mark an increase compared to previous rates. The flat rate tax burden is determined by local governments, with the prescribed ranges depending on the category of the tourist development index of the area where the property is located.

Several jurisdictions used PIT provisions to promote housing affordability

Three countries (Hungary, Ireland, Luxembourg) and two Canadian provinces announced PIT reforms to improve the affordability of housing and rents. Ireland again extended its Help-To-Buy policy which provides PIT relief to first-time home buyers until 2029, as well as extending its temporary mortgage interest relief programme by one year. Additionally, Ireland raised its Rent Tax Credit from EUR 750 to EUR 1 000. Luxembourg introduced the possibility of paying employees younger than 30 years of age a monthly rental premium of up to EUR 1 000 which benefits from a 25% tax exemption. Luxembourg also raised the annual caps on deductible interest charges for owner-occupied housing. Denmark announced expansions of its housing job scheme, which gives a tax rebate for improvements and repairs carried out in the home. In Canada, Saskatchewan increased its first-time homebuyers tax credit by 50% while also permanently reintroducing the home renovation tax credit. Meanwhile, Manitoba increased its renters tax credit and the senior top-up, accounting for inflation.

Countries also expanded tax relief for employee benefits, with a focus on promoting sustainable transport options

A number of European jurisdictions (including Finland, Germany, Ireland, Italy, the Slovak Republic, and Slovenia) introduced or expanded the preferential tax treatment of certain employer-provided fringe benefits to promote low-emission commuting. Slovenia introduced an exemption for the employee benefit of providing the electricity to charge their personal vehicles at the employers' charging stations, as well as on the use of employer-owned bicycles and pedal-powered rickshaws. Slovenia also increased the taxable benefit rate on the private use of electric company vehicles from zero to 0.75% of the value of the vehicle per month, which still represents a preferential rate to internal combustion engine (ICE) vehicles. The Slovak Republic reduced the taxable benefit rate on the private use of electric company vehicles by half to 0.5% of the entry value per month. Meanwhile, Germany increased the maximum list price for tax relief on zero-emission company vehicles to EUR 70 000. Italy revised the share of the in-kind benefits treated as taxable income between EV, hybrid, and ICE vehicles to increase the relative benefit accorded to low-emission vehicles. Ireland introduced a tax exemption on the installation of EV charging stations at an employee's residence paid by the employer. Finland extended its temporary measure to reduce the taxable value of company zero-emission vehicles.

Additionally, countries also lowered taxes on employer-provided benefits to support employees and promote well-being. Hungary, for example, expanded its beneficial 28% rate for fringe benefits to an additional monthly maximum amount of HUF 150 000 in employer-covered housing expenses for employees under the age of 35. Similarly, Latvia raised the amount of PIT relief on employer-covered expenses to EUR 700 and extended the relief to payments regarding relocation, accommodation, and transport. Latvia also doubled the amount of PIT exemptions for employer-paid funeral benefits and childbirth benefits to EUR 500. Greece introduced a new tax exemption on voluntary nursery and childcare benefits paid by employers to the parents of newborn children. Korea similarly exempted corporate childbirth support payments. Ireland introduced a EUR 10 000 deduction on the value of cars and vans for the calculation of taxable in-kind benefits. Kenya raised the exempt amounts of meal and non-cash benefits from KES 48 000 to KES 60 000 and from 36 000 to KES 60 000, respectively.

Box 3.3. Chile's 2024 Tax Compliance Reform

In October 2024, Chile enacted one of its most comprehensive tax compliance reforms. The reform package introduced a wide range of administrative measures aimed at curbing tax evasion and avoidance, enhancing transparency, and reducing informality. Key measures included:

- Strengthening the General Anti-Avoidance Rule (GAAR) by codifying definitions related to tax avoidance, establishing a committee to assess its application and raising the threshold for when the GAAR can be applied.
- Reforming penalty rules, including a new calculation method for penalties for late payments and higher penalties for various tax offences and infractions.
- Expediting the administration's access to bank account information if prior judicial authorization is obtained.
- Introducing the concept of whistleblowers in the legislation.
- Stricter rules on cash transactions, requiring identification of the payer for transactions above a specified threshold.
- New obligations on business groups, including the designation of an agent responsible for coordination with the tax authority.
- Aligning with international standards on transfer pricing and controlled foreign corporation (CFC) rules.
- Modifying the criteria for designating a foreign jurisdiction as a preferential tax regime.
- Clarifying beneficial ownership under Chile's indirect transfer tax rules, particularly in relation to capital gains realised through tax haven jurisdictions.
- Implementing a new VAT regime for low-value imports.
- Amending the luxury goods tax introduced in 2023 to clarify definitions (e.g. for yachts).
- Strengthening valuation rules across tax categories by permitting adjustments where declared values deviate significantly from market values.
- Broadening the VAT base by enabling the tax administration to assess VAT on fixed asset transfers occurring as part of corporate reorganisations, when the primary motive of such reorganisations is to avoid VAT liability.
- Introducing a temporary asset regularisation scheme, allowing taxpayers to declare previously undeclared foreign assets. The regime is limited to assets not held in high-risk or non-cooperative jurisdictions and excludes taxpayers under audit or criminal proceedings.

Source: Annual OECD Tax Policy Reform Questionnaire

Incentives to attract skilled foreign workers continued to expand

Several countries expanded their preferential tax schemes for high-skilled or high-paid foreign workers. Luxembourg, for example, significantly revised its highly skilled workers regime. Where previously specific employer-paid expenses were tax-exempt, the new regime introduces an 'impatriation premium' of up to EUR 400 000 annually that benefits from a 50% tax exemption over a maximum period of eight years. Luxembourg also introduced a new tax credit of up to EUR 700 annually for overtime hours by cross-border workers. Meanwhile, Slovenia introduced a new 7% tax credit on the salary of employees under 40 that had not been residents for the past two consecutive years and earn at least 200% of the average wage. Denmark lowered the required earnings threshold for eligibility to the gross tax scheme for foreign researchers and highly-paid employees from DKK 75 100 to DKK 60 100 per month. Sweden announced a reduction in the required monthly salary threshold for its foreign expert tax regime from SEK 117 600 to SEK 88 200 in 2025. The Netherlands reversed the decision to gradually phase out the partial tax exemption on income of skilled foreign employees and instead lowered the exemption rate by 3 percentage points to 27%. To account for the budgetary impact of this change, the salary threshold to be eligible for the expat regime increased from EUR 46 107 EUR to EUR 50 436 EUR.

Tax relief for young workers became more prominent

Some countries introduced reforms lowering the tax burden on young workers. Portugal significantly reinforced its tax exemption programme on income earned by young people, raising the maximum age to 35 years, the maximum duration of the benefit to 10 years, and the annual earnings threshold by around EUR 8 000. All income up to EUR 28 738 is fully exempt in the first year, with the exemption rate progressively decreasing to 25% for the final 3 years of the 10-year period. Meanwhile, Denmark announced an exemption from the labour market contribution, a universal earned income tax at an 8% rate, for individuals younger than 18 years old. Luxembourg introduced a premium for young employees, 75% of which are exempted from PIT, ranging between EUR 2 500 and EUR 5 000. The premium is available for five years to employees under 30 years old taking up employment in Luxembourg for the first time and earning less than EUR 100 000. Türkiye introduced a PIT exemption on income from commercial, agricultural or professional activities up to the upper threshold of the second tax bracket for first-time taxpayers younger than 29 years of age.

3.2.4. The number of countries introducing capital income tax reforms increased modestly, but most of the measures remained limited in scope

Two countries (Canada, United Kingdom) announced reforms to their taxation of capital gains. To raise additional revenues whilst ensuring the UK tax system remains internationally competitive, the United Kingdom increased its main capital gains tax rates from 10% and 20% to 18% and 24%, respectively. Additionally, it was announced that the rate of capital gains tax relief for entrepreneurs (Business Asset Disposal Relief) and on shares in non-listed trading companies (Investors' Relief) would increase in phases by 8 percentage points to 18%. The lifetime limit for Investors' Relief was also lowered from GBP 10 million to GBP 1 million, aligning the limits on both relief programmes. The higher rate on capital gains from residential property decreased by 4 percentage points to 24%. Canada announced an increase in the capital gains inclusion rate from one-half to two-thirds on the portion of realised gains exceeding CAD 250 000 but then rescinded it before it could take effect. At the same time, the Lifetime Capital Gains Exemption on the sale of small business shares and farming and fishing property would increase to CAD 1.25 million. This measure was not rescinded. Lastly, Canada announced further reforms to its Alternative Minimum Tax (AMT) on high-income individuals, primarily consisting of an exemption from AMT for certain types of trusts and allowing more deductions and tax credits under the Amt than previously announced, either fully or in part. Meanwhile, the province of Ontario has announced a reduction of its AMT rate to offset the previous year's increase in the federal rate and ensure its effective AMT remains unchanged.

Several countries made changes to the taxation of other forms of personal capital income. Israel introduced a 2% surtax on annual capital income exceeding NIS 720 000, excluding capital gains on residential property. Spain increased the highest marginal tax rate on income from savings exceeding EUR 300 000 by two percentage points to 30%. Latvia implemented an additional 3% rate on total taxable income above EUR 200 000, expanding the tax base to include certain types of capital income that in the general case are still tax exempt, such as dividends, income equivalent to dividends, conditional dividends, and liquidation quotas. Türkiye raised its withholding tax on dividend payments from 10% to 15%, and also increased withholding rates on income from various financial instruments, including investment fund participation certificates and asset- and mortgage-backed securities. In contrast, the Slovak Republic reduced its withholding tax on dividends by 3 percentage points to 7%, effective in 2026. The Netherlands reversed a previous increase in the top marginal rate on income from substantial business interests (box 2), lowering it by two percentage points to 31%. Lastly, Montenegro introduced a new tax on the proceeds from gambling, including non-traditional forms like betting on e-sports events, which will be taxed at the top PIT rate of 15%.

Greece and Luxembourg introduced changes to the taxation of income from residential property with the intention of easing the housing market pressures. Luxembourg temporarily halved the tax rate on capital gains from real estate transactions, applying 25% instead of 50% of the global personal income tax rate relevant to the taxpayer. It also introduced exemptions for capital gains on properties classified in the highest energy efficiency category or used for social rental management. Additionally, Luxembourg increased the exemption rate on rental income from properties rented through a social rental management organisation from 75% to 90%. In Greece, a three-year tax exemption was introduced for income from the rental of immovable property that had previously been declared vacant or was only available for short-term lease. Greece also extended its temporary suspension of capital gains taxation on real estate transactions.

Some European countries made changes to the taxation of savings. Lithuania introduced a preferential tax regime for specified investment accounts on which PIT applies only to withdrawn returns that exceed total deposits. On the other hand, Lithuania removed reliefs for long-term savings products by abolishing tax deductions for contributions to investment life insurance and pension accumulation. Denmark raised the cap of deposits in stock savings accounts, returns on which benefit from a preferential 17% tax rate, from DKK 135 900 to DKK 166 200. Sweden announced the introduction of tax-exempt threshold for savings in investment savings accounts and in endowment insurance.

Several countries made reforms to pension taxation. Uruguay reduced the first bracket rate of the social security assistance tax on pension income by 2 percentage points to 8%. As part of a broader pension reform, Belgium introduced a tax-exempt pension bonus for individuals that continue working past their earliest possible retirement age. The bonus can be accrued for a maximum period of three years and can amount to can amount to a net one-off bonus of up to EUR 33 975. Germany adjusted the rate at which the taxable share of pension income will increase. Where the taxable share previously increased by 1 percentage points every year (and would have reached 100% by 2040), it will now increase by 0.5 percentage points annually and reach 100% in 2058. Latvia raised the annual non-taxable minimum for pensioners by EUR 6 000 to EUR 12 000. Similarly, Romania increased the non-taxable minimum for pension income from LEI 2 000 to LEI 3 000. Meanwhile, Finland decreased the maximum net taxable earned income threshold to be eligible for the pension income deduction from EUR 55 927 to EUR 48 930. Finally, Sweden also announced tax reductions on pension income.

Some jurisdictions introduced base narrowing measures targeted at specific asset categories. To move into alignment with the EU Markets in Crypto-Assets (MiCA) framework, Czechia announced a tax exemption of long-term holdings in cryptocurrencies and digital assets, such that their tax treatment is in line with other financial assets. Macau (China) implemented a temporary tax exemption of investment income on bonds issued in the region. Ireland extended its temporary tax deductions for farmers on increases in the value of farm trading stock.

Table 3.3. Changes to tax rates on personal capital income

	Rate increase		Rate decrease	
	2023	2024 or later	2023	2024 or later
Dividend or interest income/equity or bond investment	CAN, NLD, TUR	ESP, ISR, LVA, TUR		NLD, SVK, ROU
Capital gains	AUS[1], CAN, NLD	CAN, ESP, GBR, ISR, LVA		GBR, LUX[2]
Rental income	CAN, NLD	HRV		
Tax treatment of pensions and savings account	AUS		NOR, SWE	URY

Note: 1 denotes announcement, 2 denotes a temporary reform
Source: OECD Annual Tax Policy Reform Questionnaire

Table 3.4. Changes to personal capital income tax bases

	Base broadening		Base narrowing	
	2023	2024 or later	2023	2024 or later
Dividend or interest income/equity or bond investment	CAN, NLD	LVA	CAN, DNK, MAC[1], NLD	CAN, MAC
Capital gains	AUS[2], CAN, NLD, SWE	GBR	CAN, BGR	CAN, CZE, LUX
Rental income	CAN, NLD		CAN, LUX	CAN, GRC, LUX
Tax treatment of pensions and savings account	NOR	FIN, URY	BRB, CAN, KEN, LUX1, NIG, URY	BEL, CAN, DEU, DNK, LTU, LVA
Other		MNE		

Note: 1 denotes a temporary reform, 2 includes policies that have been announced but not yet enforced
Source: OECD Annual Tax Policy Reform Questionnaire.

3.2.5. More jurisdictions raised SSC rates than lowered them while SSC base reforms were more balanced

Jurisdictions mostly introduced increases to SSC rates, while changes to SSC bases were more balanced between broadening and narrowing measures. Rate increases and base broadening measures primarily sought to raise revenues and address equity concerns. Base narrowing measures were mainly introduced to support employment. Decreases to SSC rates continued to be rare.

Jurisdictions raised SSC rates to improve the financial sustainability of their social security systems

Several countries increased their SSC rates to raise overall contribution levels. The United Kingdom announced an increase in the employer SSC rate from 13.8% to 15%. New Zealand increased contributions to its personal injury compensation scheme by 5% for employers and employees, with further increases set to occur in the next two years. Greece raised SSCs for self-employed workers by 2.7%. Israel raised their reduced SSC rate, which applies below 60% of the average wage, by 1.6 percentage points. For salaried employees, employers pay 60% of the increase and the employee pays the remaining 40%. Germany raised the average supplemental contribution to statutory health insurance, which is evenly split between employees and employers, by 0.4 percentage points to 1.25%. The standard contribution rate to long-term care insurance also increased by 0.1 percentage points to 1.8%. The Netherlands increased the employer contribution rates for its general unemployment fund by 0.1 percentage points for both permanent and flexible contracts. Additionally, the Netherlands raised employer contributions to its occupational disability insurance fund and the work reintegration fund. Guernsey raised the contribution rates by 0.1 percentage points to 7.0% for employers, by 0.2 percentage points, to 7.4%, for employees, and by 0.3 percentage points to 12.2% for self-employed people. Slovenia changed the breakdown of pension contribution rates, transferring one percentage point from the funded second pillar to the unfunded first pillar.

Three countries reduced SSC rates to support employment. Montenegro reduced the employee SSC rate by 10.5 percentage points to 10% and eliminated SSCs for employers (previously at 5.5%). Norway lowered the employee and self-employed SSC rates by 0.1 percentage points to 7.7% and 10.9%, respectively. The United Kingdom lowered National Insurance contribution rates for employees (class 1) and self-employed individuals with profits over GBP 12 570 (class 4) by 2 percentage points.

Table 3.5. Changes to social security contribution rates

	Rate increase		Rate decrease	
	2023	2024 or later	2023	2024 or later
Employer SSCs	AIA, CZE, DEU, NLD, SWE, SVK, SVN[2]	DEU, GBR, GGY, ISR, NLD, NZL	BIH	GRC, MNE
Employee SSCs	AIA, CZE, DEU, SVN[2]	DEU, GGY, ISR, NZL	BIH, DEU, GBR, NOR[4], ITA[1],	GBR, GRC, MNE, NOR[4]
Self-employed	AIA, GRC	GGY, GRC, ISR	NOR4, GBR	GBR, NOR[4]
Payroll taxes	DEU, SVN, SWE	CAN[2]	HRV	

Note: 1 denotes a temporary reform, 2 includes policies that have been announced but not yet enforced, 3 denotes that tax reform was implemented at the sub-central level, 4 as noted before for Norway the combined marginal tax rate for SSC and PIT remained unchanged for brackets three to five.
Source: OECD Annual Tax Policy Reform Questionnaire.

Meanwhile, SSC base reforms focused on employment incentives and equity considerations

Several countries implemented SSC base broadening measures. The Slovak Republic increased the maximum assessment base for all SSCs from 7 times the average wage (two years prior to the given fiscal year) to 11 times the average wage. Greece raised the ceiling on earnings subject to employees and employer SSCs by 2.7%. Hungary halved the application period of the social contribution tax allowance for new labour market entrants to a total of 18 months. Latvia raised the maximum annual amount subject to SSCs to EUR 105 300. Spain adjusted the maximum social security contribution base to the growth in the statutory minimum wage. Additionally, in 2023 Spain introduced a new solidarity contribution, which entered into force 1 January, 2025. The contribution consists of progressive rates between 0.92% and 1.17% on income exceeding the maximum base for the standard contribution. Bulgaria implemented increases to the minimum and maximum amounts of insurance incomes on which social security contributions are levied for employees, employers, and the self-employed. The United Kingdom lowered the annual salary threshold at which employers start paying SSCs from GBP 9 100 to GBP 5 000. At the same time, the employment allowance is increased from GBP 5 000 to GBP 10 500 and the maximum contribution threshold is removed such that all employers become eligible.

Some jurisdictions introduced SSC base narrowing measures to support specific types of employment. Poland introduced an optional exemption on SSCs for sole proprietors with fewer than 10 employees for one selected calendar month per year. Additionally, Poland removed revenues from sale of certain fixed assets from the base for calculating health insurance contributions for sole proprietors and temporarily reduced the minimum health insurance contribution base from 100% to 75% of the minimum wage. Portugal excluded voluntary payouts in the form of productivity bonuses, performance bonuses, or profit-sharing of up to 6% of the employee's base salary from the SSC base. The Slovak Republic introduced an SSC allowance for seasonal workers in restaurants, hospitality, and accommodation services to avoid workforce shortages in these sectors. Meanwhile, Sweden extended its employer SSC reduction for the first person employed. Belgium introduced a pension bonus for individuals working past their earliest possible retirement age (see above) which is exempted from social security contributions.

In Canada, British Columbia introduced a series of changes to one of its payroll taxes. British Columbia raised the exemption threshold for the employer health tax from CAN 500 000 to CAN 1 million. At the same time, the lower rate for remuneration above the exemption threshold and below the full rate threshold of CAN 1.5 million increases from 2.925% to 5.850%.

Table 3.6. Changes to social security contribution and payroll tax bases

	Base broadening		Base narrowing	
	2023	2024 or later	2023	2024 or later
Employer SSCs	BGR, AUS, GRC	BGR, ESP, GBR, GRC, HUN, SVK	ARG[1]	GBR, SWE
Employee SSCs	BGR, CZE, ROU, SVN, GRC	BGR, ESP, GRC, SVK		BEL, NOR, SVK
Self-employed	BGR, GRC	BGR, ESP, GRC, SVK		POL
Payroll taxes				CAN1

Note: 1 denotes that tax reform was implemented at the sub-central level.
Source: OECD Annual Tax Policy Reform Questionnaire.

3.3. Corporate income taxes and other corporate taxes

Revenue mobilisation was a key driver of CIT reform, alongside efforts to stimulate growth and investment. Questionnaire responses indicated that raising revenue was the most common objective behind recent corporate tax reforms. However, many jurisdictions also aimed to promote economic recovery, boost private sector investment, and support innovation and employment. This reflects the trade-off policymakers face in balancing the need for fiscal consolidation with the imperative to stimulate long-term growth.

For the second consecutive year in a row, CIT rate increases were more common than decreases, further suggesting that the downward trend in CIT rates has halted or is showing signs of reversing. While the past two decades were marked by declining statutory CIT rates globally, 2023 and 2024 saw a reversal of this trend. More countries raised CIT rates than reduced them, and the rate increases tended to be of greater magnitude than the decreases. A number of countries have also introduced or increased additional taxes (or surtaxes) on corporate income in order to raise revenues for the general budget in light of increased government expenditures and defence spending in particular.

Despite the rise in CIT rates, CIT base narrowing measures remain more prevalent. Countries continued to adopt base narrowing measures to provide preferential tax treatment for certain types of investment, particularly in research and development (R&D), emission-reducing technologies, and sectors considered important for national security. With statutory tax rates at historic lows, questionnaire responses suggest that countries are choosing base narrowing measures rather than rate decreases where they choose to offer more favourable CIT treatment to companies.

The trend of governments using CIT incentives to encourage environmentally friendly investment decisions and to support the transition to less carbon-intensive technologies continued in 2024. Many countries introduced or expanded tax credits for environmentally friendly investment, often through enhanced deductions or refundable credits. These incentives are typically expenditure-based and more prevalent in high- and upper-middle-income countries.

3.3.1. Wide disparities in CIT revenue shares persist across countries

CIT revenues have increased as a share of total tax revenues across all income groups since 2000, with particularly strong growth in LICs and MICs. In LICs, the average CIT share rose from around 13.2% in 2000 to over 22% in 2022. Similarly, MICs saw an increase from 11.3% to nearly 20% over the same period. In HICs the increase has been more modest, with the CIT share rising from 11.2% in 2000 to 13.3% in 2022. However, this still represents a noticeable uptick compared to 2019 levels. The disparity across countries and income groups in CIT revenues as a share of total tax revenues can be attributed to several factors, including differences in statutory CIT rates, the size of the CIT base, the prevalence of corporate entities within a jurisdiction, and the degree to which countries raise revenues from alternative taxes.

Wide disparities in CIT revenues as a share of total tax revenues remain across countries. In 2022, CIT accounted for less than 5% of total tax revenues in Latvia, Hungary, and Estonia, while exceeding 20% in countries such as Ireland, Australia, Mexico, Chile, and Colombia. Norway stands out with the highest CIT share at 42.3%, mainly due to due to exceptional profits in the energy industry in 2022 with high energy prices, which increased CIT revenues from both standard corporate taxation and special income taxes on petroleum and hydroelectric power companies.

Figure 3.3. Revenues from corporate income tax in OECD countries, 2000, 2019, 2022

CIT revenues as a percentage of total tax revenues

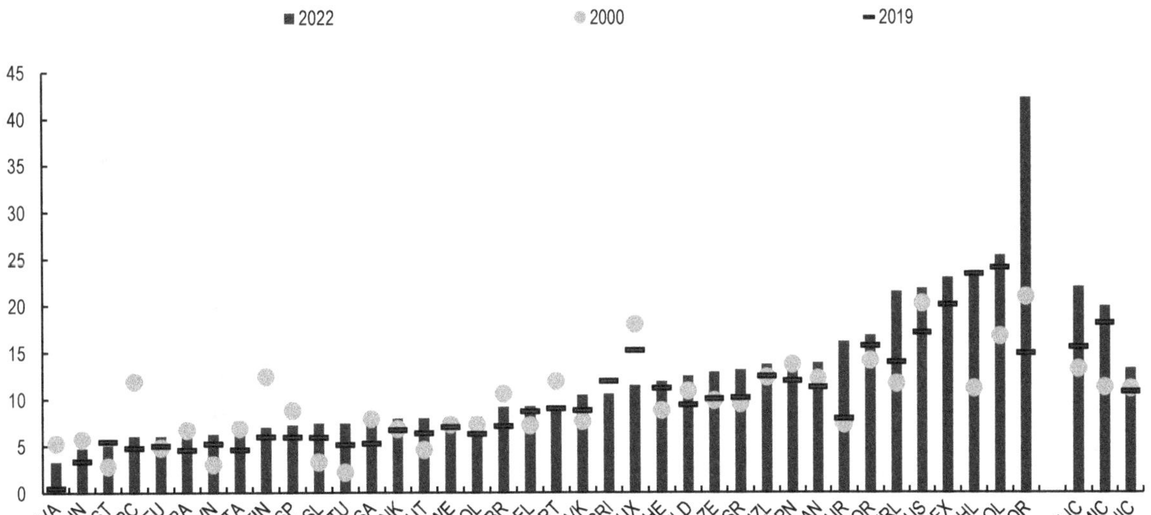

Note: Corporate income tax revenues refer to tax category 1200 under the OECD classification of taxes. Tax revenues are the sum of taxes collected by all levels of government. See Revenue Statistics Interpretative Guide for more detail. The low- (LIC), middle- (MIC), and high-income country (HIC) averages are representative of the 120 countries that provide tax revenue data to the OECD. For Norway, the CIT revenues include both ordinary CIT and special taxes on hydroelectric and petroleum revenue.
Source: OECD Global Revenue Statistics Database

StatLink https://stat.link/3yfh7u

Box 3.4. Corporate Tax Statistics 2024

First launched in 2019 as a key outcome of Action 11, the sixth edition of the Corporate Tax Statistics report was published in 2024 covering over 160 jurisdictions. This new edition includes CbC report data on the activities of more than 8 000 MNEs based on reporting from more than 50 jurisdictions. The data also includes new country-by-country data on the variation of MNEs' effective tax rates within jurisdictions, highlighting the presence of low-taxed profit in high-tax jurisdictions, which may reflect the use of tax incentives and other targeted concessions. These low-taxed profits point to the revenue-raising potential of the global minimum tax, even in jurisdictions often considered to be high-tax.

Source: OECD (2024[1]), Corporate Tax Statistics 2024, OECD Publishing, Paris,

3.3.2. *More countries increased standard and special CIT rates to raise revenues*

Standard corporate income tax rates

Statutory CIT rate increases have become more common than decreases, although overall rates remain historically low (OECD, 2023[2]). The average combined CIT rate across 143 jurisdictions covered in the OECD Corporate Tax Statistics Database was 21.1% in 2024, down from 28.0% in 2000, but no longer on a steady downward trend (Figure 3.5). In 2023 and 2024, more jurisdictions raised CIT rates than lowered them, reversing a trend observed over the past two decades.

Figure 3.4. Distribution of jurisdictions by combined statutory CIT rates

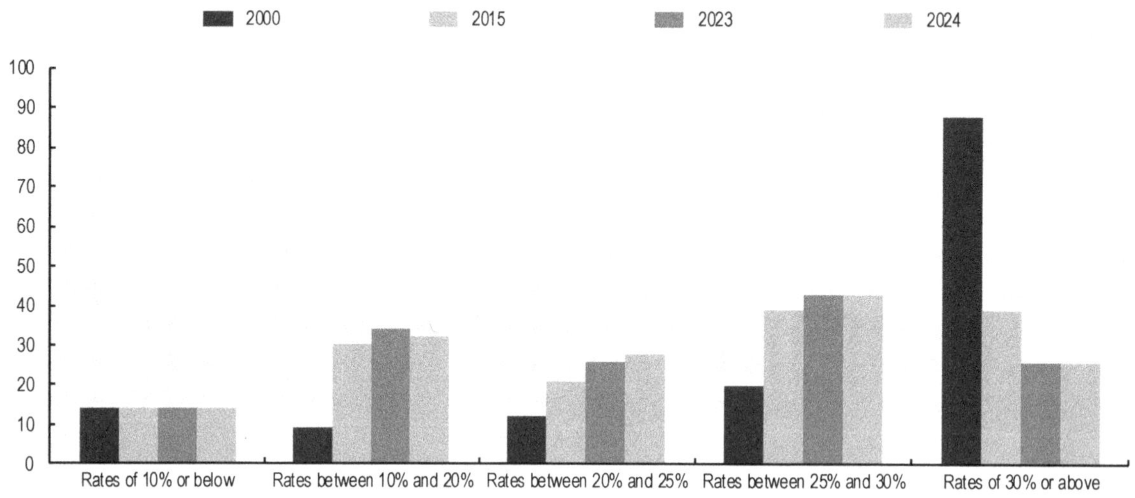

Note: Data were available for 143 OECD/G20 Inclusive Framework jurisdictions in 2024.
Source: OECD Corporate Tax Statistics Database

StatLink https://stat.link/pef6tz

Only three countries introduced a standard CIT rate cut in 2024, and none by over 1 percentage point. Austria reduced its CIT rate for 2024 to 23%, which is a further decrease from 24% in 2023 and 25% before 2023. Portugal reduced its standard CIT rate from 21% to 20%. Luxembourg also lowered its CIT rates, reducing the higher standard rate from 17% to 16% and the reduced rate for smaller businesses from 15% to 14%. Meanwhile, Italy introduced a targeted CIT incentive reducing the CIT rate for companies meeting specific conditions related to reinvestment and employment from 24% to 20%. To qualify, firms must retain at least 80% of their 2024 profits for three years, invest a portion of these profits in eligible Transition 4.0 or 5.0 assets, and increase employment by at least 1% compared to the previous year.

Meanwhile, five (Czechia, Iceland, Slovenia, the Slovak Republic, and Lithuania) jurisdictions implemented or introduced CIT rate increases in 2024 to raise additional revenues. These CIT rate increases were substantial, with three of the five countries raising the rate by at least 2 percentage points. Czechia increased their standard rates by 2 percentage points, from 19% to 21%. Iceland temporarily raised its CIT rate from 20% to 21% for 2024. Slovenia temporarily increased its CIT rate by 3 percentage points from 19% to 22% for five years starting in 2024. The Slovak Republic also increased its CIT rate by 3 percentage points from 21% to 24% for companies with taxable income over EUR 5 million. Meanwhile Lithuania increased its standard CIT rate from 15% to 16% and its preferential rate from 5% to 6% as part of a defence fund package.

Table 3.7. Changes in corporate income tax rates

	Rate increase		Rate decrease	
	2023	2024 or later	2023	2024 or later
Standard CIT rate	ARE, COL, EST, ROU, TUR	CZE, ISL, LTU, SVN, SVK	CUW	PRT, AUT, LUX
SME CIT rate	ROU	BRB, JPN[2]	CAN[1], CHL	ARM, ESP, PRT, SVK
Mining	CHL	IMN		

Note: Countries in brackets are those that have announced reforms but are yet to implement them.
1. The CIT rate decrease in Canada, announced in 2021 at the federal level, applies to zero-emission technology manufacturing profits, reducing the general corporate income tax rate and small business income tax rate on eligible profits to 7.5% (from 15%) and to 4.5% (from 9%), respectively, for taxation years beginning after 2021 and before 2029. 2. The SME CIT rate increase from 15% to 17% in Japan applies only to SMEs with annual taxable income of over JPY 1 billion.
Source: OECD Annual Tax Policy Reform Questionnaire.

New or higher CIT rates were also introduced in response to international tax developments. Barbados, which previously did not have a CIT system in place, implemented its 9% CIT rate as of January 1, 2024, alongside a preferential 5.5% rate for small businesses and a 4.5% patent box regime. The preferential rate applies from the 2024 fiscal year to companies registered as small businesses[2] with a gross income below USD 2 million (EUR 1.8 million).

CIT rates for Small and Medium-Sized Enterprises

Changes in SME tax rates were mixed, with several jurisdictions cutting rates (Portugal, the Slovak Republic, and Spain). Portugal, Spain, and the Slovak Republic introduced reductions to support SMEs, often through tiered or progressive rate structures. Portugal reduced its corporate income tax rate for SMEs on the first EUR 50 000 of taxable income from 17% to 16%, and 12.5% for eligible startups. The Slovak Republic increased the eligibility threshold for its reduced tax rate for small firms from income below EUR 60 000 to EUR 100 000 and further reduced the rate to 10% (from 15% previously. Spain reduced CIT rates for small enterprises through a tiered rate structure. For firms with net income under EUR 1 million, the rate was cut from 23% to 17% on the first EUR 50 000 of taxable income and 20% on the remainder. The reductions will be phased in between 2025 and 2026, with the standard SME rate also set to gradually decline from 24% in 2025 to 21% in 2028.

Meanwhile, two countries (Armenia and Japan) increased their special tax rates for SMEs. Armenia increased the tax rate on SMEs from 5% to 10%, and transitioned specific professional services, including legal and accounting firms, from a turnover tax system to the general taxation system. Japan maintained its special corporate tax rate of 15% for two additional years, while also increasing the tax rate for SMEs with annual taxable income of over JPY 1 billion to 17%.

Other business taxes

In 2024, over 10 countries (including the Belgium, Hungary, Ireland, Isle of Man, Israel, Mauritius, the Netherlands, the Slovak Republic, Spain and Ukraine – introduced or increased taxes targeting banks and other financial institutions. These taxes are typically levied in addition to standard corporate income tax and may apply to different tax bases. Ukraine made the CIT rate of 25% for financial institutions (excluding insurers) permanent and applied a 50% rate on bank profits, including dividends, for the 2024 tax year. Israel imposed an additional 6% tax on the profits of large banks from April 2024 through the end of 2025. Hungary extended its extraordinary bank tax through 2025, with rates set at 7% on the portion of the base up to HUF 20 billion and 18% above that threshold. Mauritius eliminated a preferential 5% tax rate previously available to banks. Latvia applies its previously announced 20% annual CIT surcharge for credit institutions and consumer credit providers and in addition Latvia introduced a temporary solidarity levy on credit institutions, effective from 2025 to 2027. The solidarity contribution applies a 60% rate on net interest income that exceeds the institutions five-year average net interest income by over 50%. The measure also provides for the possibility of a rebate depending on how significantly the credit institution increases its credit volumes. Additionally – as covered in the previous edition of the report – Lithuania continued to levy a temporary solidarity contribution payable by credit institutions from May 2023 to June 2025, and Slovenia also continued to apply its 0.2% tax on banks' total assets, capped at 30% of operating profits, for the period 2024 to 2028.

Some countries have introduced broader surtaxes or special CIT rules to target retained earnings or undistributed profits. Israel introduced a new law regarding the taxation of undistributed profits commencing January 1, 2025. Labour-intensive companies that were previously taxed at a reduced rate of 23% on profits (CIT) and 30% to 33% on dividends will now have profits exceeding 25% of turnover taxed at the marginal rate (up to 50%). The tax will apply on companies with accumulated profits exceeding NIS 750 000 and a turnover of up to NIS 30 million multiplied by the number of significant shareholders. Furthermore, holding companies will have an additional annual tax of 2%, imposed on accumulated retained earnings that exceed certain thresholds.

Governments also adopted new corporate taxes or surtaxes to raise revenues, especially to finance defence spending. Ukraine increased its military tax rate on corporate income from 1.5% to 5%. Estonia introduced a Security Tax of 2% on corporate income that will apply from 2026 to 2028 to raise additional tax revenues for defence expenditures. Similarly, Japan announced a new 4% surtax starting in April 2026 on CIT liability (equivalent to approximately a 1% CIT rate) after deducting JPY 5 million. In Romania, an additional 1% tax on turnover entered into force from January 2024 for companies that had turnover over EUR 50 million in the previous fiscal year and a tax liability lower than the minimum tax in the current fiscal year.

Several jurisdictions have also adjusted corporate tax policy in the extractives and energy sectors to raise additional revenue. Colombia increased its withholding tax rates on all income, with a particular focus on income from oil and coal. Norway introduced a new resource rent tax on onshore wind farms, structured as a cash flow tax with immediate expensing of new investments. Lastly, Isle of Man introduced a 20% CIT rate specifically on petroleum extraction activities.

Lastly, the Slovak Republic reduced the CIT rate on income from government bonds to 16% in 2025, with a further reduction to 13% planned for 2026, aiming to enhance the attractiveness of government bonds for domestic investors.

Intellectual property regimes

None of the jurisdictions that responded to the tax policy reforms questionnaire reported altering the tax rates applied to intellectual property (IP) regimes in 2024. As has been the trend for a number of years, jurisdictions have modified IP regime bases (OECD, 2023[3]). Five IP regimes were reviewed in 2024 (OECD, 2023[3]) as part of the BEPS Action 5 peer review process, three of which were found to be non-harmful (Barbados, Hong Kong and Trinidad and Tobago), one was abolished (Trinidad and Tobago) and one remains under review (Malaysia).

3.3.3. CIT base narrowing reforms remained prevalent and focused on investment and innovation

As has been the case since the first edition of the tax policy reforms report, the number of base narrowing measures adopted in 2024 exceeded the number of base broadening measures. Jurisdictions commonly cited boosting growth, stimulating investment (especially in more environmentally friendly technologies), and encouraging innovation as reasons for reforms.

Table 3.8. Changes to corporate tax bases

	Base broadening		Base narrowing	
	2023	2024 or later	2023	2024 or later
Capital allowances and general incentives	BEL, BEN, COL, MKD, NLD	AUS, BEL, LTU, NLD, NZL, MYS, NGA	GBR, ITA, JPN, LVA, MAC, MEX, MYS, NOR, PER, PRT, TUR, URY	AUS, BEL, BRB, CAN, DNK, ESP, GBR, GRC, JPN, KEN, MAC, MUS, MEX, MNE, PER, PRT, SVN, TUR,
Environmentally related tax incentives			ESP, FRA, IRL, MYS, PER, ZAF	AUS, BEL, BRB, CAN, CZE, ESP, FRA, GBR, HUN, IRL, MYS, PER, ZAF
R&D tax incentives and patent box regimes			GBR, IRL, SGP	ARM, BRB, DNK, GBR, GRC, JPN, MAC
SME-related tax base changes	PER, ROU	PER, ROU	DEU, FRA, GBR	ALB, AUS, DEU, FRA, GBR, GRC, JPN, KOR, NGA
Other business tax incentives	ALB, MUS, KEN	ALB, MUS, KEN	ESP, BRB, HRV, KEN, MYS, PER, TTO	AUS, BRB, ESP, IRL, MEX, HRV, KEN, MUS, MYS, PER, TTO
Loss carryforward and carryback provisions		NAM	KOR	DNK, GRC
Notional interest deductions		ITA, NAM		NLD

Note: Countries in brackets have only announced reforms.
Source: OECD Annual Tax Policy Reform Questionnaire.

Capital allowances and general tax incentives

Jurisdictions also aimed to stimulate investment and boost growth via new or more generous tax incentives. In Portugal, the amount of the allowance for corporate equity was increased by 50% in 2025, providing businesses with greater flexibility to use retained earnings for investment purposes. Greece enhanced its tax incentives for angel investors to stimulate start-up financing and innovation. The maximum deductible amount from taxable income was tripled – from EUR 300 000 to EUR 900 000 – covering up to 50% of the capital invested in start-ups. Belgium reformed its investment allowance regime, adjusting the conditions under which businesses can claim deductions to better target productive investments. Barbados announced a broad range of investment-related tax credits targeting health, education, sports, and national development projects. These include up to 75% tax credits for qualifying special needs education facilities, 50% credits for sports and entertainment venues, and refundable credits for strategic projects aligned with the National Development Strategy. Montenegro introduced a package of sector-targeted corporate tax incentives under its 2024 – 2027 Fiscal Strategy. These include exemptions for reinvested profits in agricultural businesses, tax recognition for contributions to national sports associations (up to 5% of revenue), and the removal of restrictions on tax exemptions for new agricultural and fisheries operations in underdeveloped municipalities. Mexico granted an immediate 100% deduction for original investments made in certain industrial zones for the first six years of operation, aiming to accelerate industrial development in these strategic regions.

Some jurisdictions introduced more favourable tax treatment for specific types of expenses and assets, often in support of non-tax policy objectives. Australia, for example, introduced measures aimed to support an increase in rental housing supply, including affordable housing by updating its policies to accelerate tax deductions and reduce managed investment trust withholding tax rates for Build-to-Rent housing developments. This is aimed at increasing the supply of rental (including affordable) housing and providing better protections for renters. Another example is Latvia, which introduced a law that categorises expenses on fuel and luxury cars as business expenses if the car has been in the taxpayer's possession for over 60 months, from 1 January 2024. Previously, all costs associated with luxury vehicles were considered non-business expenses, treated as a profit distribution[3], and therefore subject to a 20% tax rate

Some jurisdictions increased the stringency of its tax allowances or removed some broadly targeted incentives to raise revenue. Australia, for example, announced a strengthened capital income tax regime for foreign residents, clarifying and broadening the types of assets that foreign residents are subject to capital gains tax on. Canada proposed to increase the capital gains inclusion rate from one-half to two-thirds for corporations but then rescinded it before it could take effect. Manitoba, Canada eliminated the Data Processing Investment Tax Credit, which had provided refundable tax credits to data processing centre corporations to offset infrastructure costs.

R&D and innovation tax incentives

A number of jurisdictions increased their support for R&D and innovation by introducing new tax incentives, increasing the generosity of existing ones, and extending the duration of others. Several jurisdictions increased the generosity of existing tax credits or extended their duration to strengthen support for business investment in innovation. Denmark raised the enhanced rate on tax allowances on R&D capital and raised the ceiling on its R&D tax credit. Ireland increased the first-year payment threshold under its R&D tax credit from EUR 50 000 to EUR 75 000, helping firms access greater upfront liquidity. In Barbados, a 50% tax credit was introduced for qualifying R&D activities, alongside a 100% credit for local businesses investing in digital transformation, signalling an emphasis on digital innovation.

Other jurisdictions introduced reforms to promote investment in cutting-edge technologies such as AI and digital infrastructure. Mauritius expanded its 15% investment tax credit to cover expenditures on artificial intelligence and patents. Similarly, Armenia introduced generous deductions for high-tech sector employees and scientific research activities, allowing companies to deduct up to 200% of related salary costs, subject to certain limits. Macau (China) also enhanced its allowable deduction for qualifying R&D expenditures under its Profits Tax regime.

Canada undertook a broad set of reforms to strengthen both federal and subnational R&D incentives. The 2024 Fall Economic Statement proposed key enhancements to the Scientific Research and Experimental Development (SR&ED) tax incentive program, including raising the annual expenditure limit eligible for the enhanced 35% investment tax credit from CAD 3 million to CAD 4.5 million and extending eligibility to capital expenditures. At the provincial level, Saskatchewan extended its patent box program by one year and expanded eligibility to start-ups developing novel technologies in the clean technology sector, Nova Scotia extended its innovation equity tax credit and its venture capital tax credit until 2029, while Quebec rebalanced its e-business development tax credit by increasing the non-refundable portion from 6% to 10% and reducing the refundable share from 24% to 20%.

Recent changes to R&D and innovation tax incentives reflect a continued trend of governments using tax policy to encourage business investment in R&D, although some evidence in recent editions of this report suggests that the pace of introducing new measures has slowed. The number of OECD countries providing income-based tax relief for R&D expenditures grew from 20 in 2000 to 31 out of 38 OECD members by 2023 (OECD, 2024[1]). Between 2000 and 2023, the average implied marginal R&D tax subsidy across OECD countries rose significantly, driven by the adoption of new incentives and the increased generosity of existing R&D tax relief mechanisms. Despite remaining well above pre-COVID-19 levels, the OECD average tax subsidy rate remained stable in 2023. On average, SMEs benefited from higher tax incentives due to the preferential tax treatment specifically aimed at smaller firms. However, there are considerable variations in the tax incentives for large, profitable companies across countries and over time. In 2023, Portugal, France, and Poland offered the most generous preferential tax treatment for profitable and marginal R&D investments. For SMEs, the highest implied marginal R&D tax subsidy rates were recorded in Iceland, Portugal, and France (OECD, 2024[1]).

Box 3.5. The challenge of reducing tax avoidance continues to be tackled through the wider OECD/G20 BEPS programme

Further progress was made on the implementation of the OECD/G20 BEPS package in 2024. The OECD/G20 BEPS package was delivered in October 2015 and includes 15 Actions aimed at addressing tax planning strategies that artificially shift profits to low or no-tax jurisdictions.

The Multilateral Convention to Implement Tax Treaty Related Measures to Prevent BEPS (BEPS MLI) has taken effect for approximately 1 600 tax agreements (OECD, 2023[4]). The BEPS MLI implements tax treaty-related BEPS measures to address hybrid mismatch arrangements (BEPS Action 2), to prevent treaty abuse (BEPS Action 6), to prevent the artificial avoidance of permanent establishment status (BEPS Action 7) and to improve dispute resolution mechanisms (BEPS Action 14). As of 1 July 2025, 105 jurisdictions have signed the BEPS MLI, out of which 89 have deposited the instrument of ratification, acceptance, or approval. Overall, the BEPS MLI now covers almost 2 000 bilateral tax agreements. This includes around 1 600 agreements that have already been modified by the BEPS MLI and around 500 additional agreements that will be modified once all Signatories ratify the BEPS MLI. These figures continue to increase as additional jurisdictions sign and ratify the BEPS MLI.

Successive BEPS Action 6 peer review reports demonstrate a broadly successful implementation of the minimum standard on treaty shopping by jurisdictions that are members of the Inclusive Framework. As one of the four minimum standards, the BEPS Action 6 minimum standard identified treaty abuse, and in particular treaty shopping, as one of the principal sources of BEPS concerns. Over the years, the BEPS Action 6 peer review reports have revealed sustained and steady progress in the implementation of the BEPS Action 6 minimum standard across the treaty networks of jurisdictions that are members of the Inclusive Framework. As revealed in the latest peer review report, the number of agreements concluded between members of the Inclusive Framework that were compliant with the minimum standard increased by around 30% in 2024 relative to 2023 (OECD, 2024[5]). Moreover, at this stage, over 95% of the agreements concluded by Inclusive Framework members (covering most of the global tax treaty network) were either already compliant or on track to becoming compliant with the minimum standard. Consistent with previous years, the sixth Peer Review Report confirms the importance of the BEPS MLI as the principal tool used by jurisdictions to implement the BEPS Action 6 minimum standard (OECD, 2024[5]). The number of bilateral agreements between members of the Inclusive Framework that comply with the minimum standard increased from only 13 agreements in 2018 to over 1 600 agreements in 2025, driven by the entry into effect of the provisions of the BEPS MLI.

In line with Action 13, automatic exchanges of country-by-country (CbC) reports have continued to increase. Action 13 requires the ultimate parent entity of an MNE group to file a CbC report in its jurisdiction, providing information such as turnover, profits, employees, and taxes paid for each of the jurisdictions in which it operates. The tax administration of the country where the ultimate parent entity is a resident, exchanges this data with the tax authorities of other jurisdictions. In September 2024, the Inclusive Framework concluded the seventh peer review report, covering 138 jurisdictions. The implementation of CbC reporting has made considerable progress since 2015, with more than 4 650 bilateral relationships for CbC exchanges now in place between 93 jurisdictions.

Action 14, which deals with mutual agreement procedures (MAP), has also seen significant progress. Action 14 aims to improve mechanisms for the resolution of tax-treaty related disputes. A new Peer Review Assessment Methodology was agreed by the Inclusive Framework to increase the efficiency of resolutions for double taxation disputes, as well as the reporting of additional data points for MAP statistics (OECD, 2023[6]). Advance Pricing Arrangement programmes will be reported in annual statistics and published online from 2024, which should facilitate the aim of achieving compliance with the Action 14 minimum standard.

Interest deductions

Reforms to interest deduction rules varied across jurisdictions, with two tightening restrictions and one providing more generous treatment. Italy abolished its allowance for corporate equity provision (ACE), effective from 2024. Previously, the ACE allowed for a deduction from taxable profit based on the net increase in equity, multiplied by a rate of 1.3%. Deductions of write-downs and losses on loans and goodwill related to DTAs (deferred tax assets) have been deferred for 2025 and 2026 tax years. Moreover, regarding the additional income due to those deferrals, a limitation in the offsetting of previous losses and previous ACE surpluses has been introduced only for 2025 tax year. Namibia introduced a new interest deduction limitation rule to curb base erosion. In contrast, the Netherlands eased its limitation on interest deductions by increasing the deduction cap from 20% to 25% of EBITDA, bringing it in line with the European average.

Environmentally related tax incentives

Some jurisdictions implemented base narrowing measures to incentivise green investment and support the transition to a lower-carbon economy. These reforms, though less widespread than in 2023, focused on promoting clean energy, low-emission transportation, and sustainability-oriented business activities. Canada reformed multiple green tax incentives, including an expansion of its Clean Hydrogen Investment Tax Credit to cover methane pyrolysis, and a new 10% Electric Vehicle Supply Chain Investment Tax Credit to support battery and EV component manufacturing. Canada's province of Quebec also refined its incentive scheme for biofuel and pyrolysis oil production, aiming to strengthen support for alternative energy sources. Similarly, Peru extended its accelerated depreciation scheme for renewable energy investments through 2030, applying an annual depreciation rate of 20% rate to qualifying installations and infrastructure. Barbados introduced a broad package of green tax credits, including a 50% refundable credit for net-zero emissions projects and marine conservation, and a 25% non-refundable credit for R&D linked to the ocean and green economy.

Other reforms focused on decarbonising transportation. Spain enhanced the generosity of its depreciation rules for investments in various electric and hydrogen vehicles and their charging infrastructure. Similarly, Ireland extended its Accelerated Capital Allowance for Gas Vehicles and Refuelling Equipment, which allows businesses to claim tax benefits for investments in low-emission transportation infrastructure, until the end of 2025. Belgium expanded its tax-exempt bicycle allowance and added a refundable credit for employers subsidising train passes, while further promoting sustainable commuting options.

SME-related tax base changes

Several jurisdictions have introduced tax reforms aimed at supporting small and medium-sized enterprises (SMEs) and fostering business growth. In Canada, Newfoundland and Labrador reduced the small business corporate tax rate from 3% to 2.5% on the first CAD 500 000 of active business income. Similarly, Saskatchewan (Canada) announced that its small business corporate tax rate, previously expected to return to 2% in mid-2024, will instead be permanently set at 1%, with corresponding adjustments to the dividend tax credit rate. In Europe, Greece lowered the minimum share capital threshold for newly formed SME collaborations from EUR 125 000 to EUR 100 000 to secure a 30% tax exemption on profits, while also introducing the ability for SMEs to carry forward tax losses from business transformations. In Poland, new regulations introduced tax relief (both in CIT and in PIT for unincorporated businesses) for employers hiring the Territorial Defence Forces and Active Reserve military personnel, with SMEs eligible for a more favourable deduction multiplier of 1.5. Additionally, Japan expanded the tax incentive for SME business enhancement, making buildings eligible assets for SMEs aiming to achieve sales of over 10 billion yen. Additionally, Japan maintained its special corporate tax rate of 15% for SMEs for two more years but increased the tax rate for SMEs with extremely high-income levels to 17%.

Singapore introduced a 50% corporate income tax rebate for all companies in the Year of Assessment 2024, capped at SGD 40 000. And, finally, Nigeria implemented a withholding tax exemption for small companies and manufacturers, aiming to ease compliance burdens and improve liquidity for SMEs.

One country introduced a significant base broadening reform in this area. Romania lowered the eligibility turnover threshold of its micro-enterprise regime from EUR 500 000 to EUR 250 000 for 2025 and to EUR 100 000 in 2026.

3.3.4. Countries continued to introduce legislation implementing the Global Minimum Tax

In 2024, countries have continued to legislate measures to implement the Global Minimum Tax (GMT). A more detailed discussion of the GMT can be found in the previous edition of this report (OECD, 2024[7]). Additionally, details on country implementation are kept in a central record of the legislation with transitional qualified status, which is published on the OECD's website (OECD, 2025[8]). The central record sets out those jurisdictions whose minimum tax legislation has completed the process for the transitional qualification mechanism and secured transitional qualified status. The central record will be updated on a regular basis and in a timely manner, after a self-certification that has been submitted to the Inclusive Framework has completed the transitional qualification mechanism process. The fact that a jurisdiction's legislation is not included in this central record does not mean that the legislation is not qualified; rather it means that, as at the date of publication, the process provided for under the transitional qualification mechanism has not yet been initiated or completed for that legislation.

3.4. Taxes on goods and services

Almost all jurisdictions continued to apply a wide variety of reduced rates with the stated aim of increasing equity or to stimulate certain sectors of the economy. In almost all jurisdictions, governments apply reduced VAT rates or exemptions, most often intended to reduce the tax burden on essential products such as food, healthcare, education and housing. Reduced VAT rates were also used as a means of supporting certain sectors, such as sports, tourism, culture and agriculture.

Many jurisdictions continued to use targeted temporary VAT rate reductions as a tool to cushion price increases on specific products or as part of support measures in response to natural disasters. After the phasing out of emergency measures implemented during and in the immediate aftermath of COVID-19, governments used temporary VAT rate cuts to mitigate the impact of the sharp price increases on essential goods such as energy and food during the energy price crisis Additionally, temporary VAT rate reductions have also been used to support sectors considered to be the most affected by economic shocks and to provide relief in the aftermath of earthquakes, hurricanes and floods.

Increasingly, jurisdictions used the VAT system to support the transition to low-carbon economies. Reduced VAT rates, and in some cases VAT exemptions, are applied to goods and services identified as promoting environmental sustainability. Many of these VAT exemptions and reduced rates (as well as subsidies) are temporary and governments regularly adjust their scope or level in response to market developments, as well as to address concerns about tax revenue loss and impacts on equity.

A number of jurisdictions increased the level of their standard VAT rate. In 2024, eight countries raised their standard VAT rate to mobilise tax revenues. While some increases reversed earlier temporary cuts, others were part of ongoing fiscal consolidation efforts.

In an ongoing effort to raise revenues and promote public health by discouraging the consumption of certain products or activities, several high and upper-middle-income countries have increased their health-related excise taxes, especially on tobacco, alcoholic beverages, sugar sweetened beverages (SSBs), and gambling. Sixteen countries have increased their excise tax burden on tobacco products. Seven countries increased their excise taxes on alcohol. Two countries introduced new taxes on SSBs. Meanwhile only three countries have reduced alcohol excise taxes to support businesses.

3.4.1. Taxes on goods and services remain the backbone of revenues in low- and middle-income countries

Taxes on goods and services continue to represent the largest source of tax revenue in LICs and MICs and remain an important revenue stream in HICs as well. In 2022, taxes on goods and services accounted for, on average, over 55% of total revenues in LICs and just over 50% in MICs. By contrast, the average share in HICs was lower, at 33.5%. While there has been a slight decline in the average share of these taxes in LICs and HICs since 2019, MICs have seen relative stability. Within this category, VAT is the main contributor to revenues. On average, VAT generated 20.8% of total tax revenue across OECD countries in 2022 – almost four times as much as excise duties, which made up 5.6%. This underscores VAT's central role in tax revenues.

There remains significant variation across countries in the share of tax revenues derived from goods and services. In 2022, taxes on goods and services represented less than 20% of total revenues in countries such as the United States, Norway, and Switzerland, while accounting for over 47% in Hungary and Chile, and over 44% in Colombia and Latvia. Several countries, including Greece, Estonia, and Türkiye, experienced increases in the share of goods and services taxes since 2000, while others, such as Korea and Norway, have seen significant declines. These differences reflect not only policy choices such as the adoption or rate-setting of VAT, but also structural factors including the size of the informal sector, consumption patterns, and reliance on other tax revenues.

Figure 3.5. Revenues from taxes on goods and services

Tax revenues from taxes on goods and services as a percentage of total tax revenues

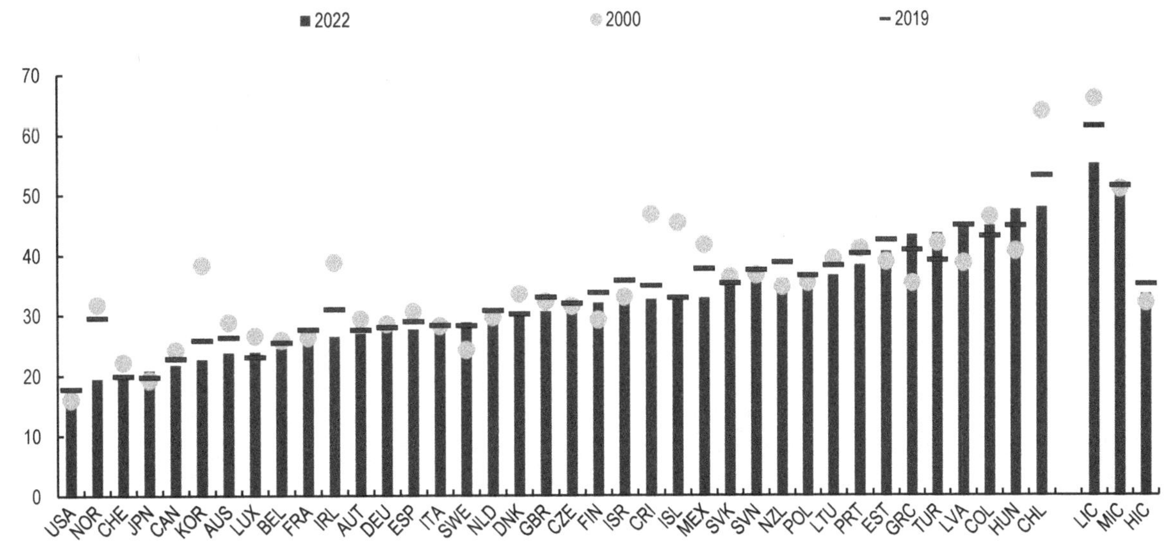

Note: Tax revenues from taxes on goods and services refer to tax category 5000 under the OECD classification of taxes. Tax revenues are the sum of taxes collected by all levels of government. See Revenue Statistics Interpretive Guide for more detail. The low- (LIC), middle- (MIC), and high-income country (HIC) averages are representative of the 116 jurisdictions that provide tax revenue data to the OECD.
Source: OECD Global Revenue Statistics Database.

StatLink https://stat.link/sgdo07

3.4.2. Reduced VAT rates continue to be used as social and economic policy tools, however countries also phased out temporary cuts as inflation eased

Most countries continued to apply reduced VAT rates or exemptions as part of a broader strategy to reduce the tax burden on essential goods and services, promote equity, and support economic activity. In fact, with the exception of Chile, all OECD countries that operate a VAT apply one or more reduced rate (OECD, 2024[9]). Thirty-five of the countries surveyed in this report have reported VAT rate changes in 2024, including 14 VAT rate increases and 39 decreases. Reduced rates on food, health, housing, energy, tourism, and culture were among the most frequently expanded in 2024.

Table 3.9. VAT rates changes in 2023 – 2024

	Reduced VAT rates			
	Increases		Decreases	
	2023	2024 or later	2023	2024 or later
Energy, Heating, Fuels		CZK, DEU, ESP,	ALB, AIA, BEL, BRB[1], BUL[1], FIN[1], DEU[1], HRV[1], IRL[1], ITA[1], KEN[1], MKD[1], PRT[1], SPA[1], UKR[1]	BRB[1], HRV[1], PRT, IRL
Food, Water, Basic essentials, Health, Housing	MKD, ROU, SVK, TUR	AUT BGR, ESP, FIN, TUR	BGR[1], COD[1], GBR, GRE, IRL, ITA, KEN, MUS, MKD, PER[1], POL[1], SPA	AIA, AUT, AZE, BEL, CAN[1], FIN, GBR, GRE, HUN, LTV[1], MUS, NOR, PRT, SAU, SVK
Hotels, Restaurants, Tourism, Passenger transport	EST, ROU	BGR, EST, FIN, MNE, SVK,	AGO[1], AUT, BGR[1], DEU[1], FIN[1], GRE, HUN, LTU, MUS, PER[1], SVK, URY	BGR[1], CAN[1], GRE, PER[1], SVK, URU[1]
Culture, Sport, and Printed & e-publications	EST, NOR, ROU	MNE, BGR, FIN	BGR[1], HUN, IRL, LVA LTU[1], PER[1], MUS, MKD, PRT, SVK	DEU, HUN, IRL, LTV, PER[1], PRT, SVK.
Agriculture			GRC, POL, PRT	ALB, IRL, MNE, MUS, POL PRT, URU
Environmental sustainability	NOR, ROU	ITA	AUT[1], BRB[1], BEL[1], DEU, GBR[1], IRL, ISL, JAM, LTU, NET, PRT, TUR	AUT[1], BEL[1], BRB[1], GBR[1], ISL[1], IRL, KOR[1], NGA[1], PRT
Mitigating effects of natural disasters/ pandemics		CAN	GRC, MEX[1], TUR[1], URY[1], AGO	GRC, MEX[1], POL[1], TUR[1]
Other		FIN, SVN, SVK,	GRC	MUS, MEX, TUR
General increase/decrease	CHE, CZE, ISL, LUX, SWE, NET[1], TUR	CZE, CHE	TUR[1], ALB, BEL, COD, IRL, JAM, LCA, POL[1], PRT[1], ROU, SVN, URY	ALB, CAN[1], CZE, MEX, PRT, TUR
	Standard VAT rates			
	Increases		Decreases	
	2023	2024 or later	2023	2024 or later
	MDV, SGP, TUR	CHE, EST, FIN, IDN, ISR, LUX, SGP, SVK	LUX	

Note: For the purposes of this table, reduced VAT rates include all rates lower than the standard rate, including zero rates applied to domestic sales. This table includes VAT rates changes adopted in 2024 either as an extension of temporary changes implemented in preceding years, new rates implemented in 2024, or adoption of changes to be implemented in 2025. Reduced VAT rate increase may mean it may mean moving from one reduced rate to another higher reduced rate or to the standard rate. "1." denotes temporary measure
Source: OECD Annual Tax Policy Reform Questionnaire.

Countries expanded reduced VAT rates on a wide range of goods and services in 2024, predominately to address cost-of living concerns

Reduced VAT rates continued to be widely used to support households and address equity concerns (OECD, 2024[9]) **by targeting essential goods and services.** In 2024, countries continued to expand the use of such reduced VAT rates on products such as food, health items, heating, and housing. Czechia, which applies reduced VAT rates to items in the areas of food, health, culture, and housing, revised its VAT rate structure by consolidating two reduced rates (10% and 15%) into a single reduced rate of 12% with the aim of simplifying the system and improving compliance. In Norway, the Government implemented targeted cost-of-living measures, including reducing the VAT rate on wastewater services and water supply from 25% to 15%. In the Slovak Republic a new reduced rate structure will also take effect from 1 January 2025. The existing 10% reduced rate was abolished, and a new reduced VAT rate of 19% applies to electricity, non-alcoholic beverages served in restaurants, and food which is not covered by the 5% rate (down from the former 20% rate). The scope of the original 5% rate is extended to a number of items that were formerly subject to the 10% reduced VAT rate (i.e. certain food items, medications and medical devices, books and e-books, accommodation and restaurant services, entrance to sports events and admission to fitness centres). In Portugal, starting 1 January 2025, the temporary 6% VAT rate on electricity consumption – previously limited to 100 kWh per month (or 150 kWh for large families) from October 2022 to December 2024 – was replaced by a permanent application of the reduced rate to contracts of 200 kWh (or 300 kWh for large families). Additionally, Portugal also reduced the VAT rate on food for small children from 13% to 6%. Anguilla reduced the VAT rate on basic food and water supply to 0%.

Other VAT reduced rate expansions related to food and beverages occurred in Austria, Hungary, and Mauritius. As of 1 August 2024, Austria, reduced its VAT rate to 0% on food donations to charitable organisations. Hungary extended its reduced VAT rate of 18% to dessert type cheese. Mauritius applied a 0% VAT rate to roasted coffee. Canada will also temporarily apply a 0% GST/HST rate from December 2024 to February 2025 on certain items, including prepared foods, restaurant meals, alcohol (excluding spirits), children's clothing and footwear, selected toys, books, and print newspapers. In Latvia, which had temporarily reduced its VAT rate on basic foods to 5% until the end of 2024, the government has decided not to return to the standard rate of 21% for fruits and vegetables. Instead, these items will be subject to a reduced rate of 12% from 1 January 2025.

Countries also continued to apply reduced VAT rates on the supply of goods and services in the area of private or social housing. In Belgium, the limited and temporary 6% reduced VAT rate introduced in 2022 for the demolition-reconstruction of housing was made permanent country-wide in January 2024 and extended in June 2024 to include the reconstruction of rental properties. Saudi Arabia extended the scope of its VAT refunds for real estate developers in May 2024 to reduce their financial burden and stimulate construction.

Goods and services related to health, hygiene, and sport also continue to benefit from reduced VAT rates in many jurisdictions, with some countries further expanding their scope. Finland joined others in reducing the VAT rate on menstrual hygiene products, and diapers from the standard rate to the 14% reduced rate. Latvia introduced a VAT exemption, effective 1 January 2024, for participation fees in sports competitions and for sports lessons provided by registered associations. Mauritius applied a 0% VAT rate to baby lotions in August 2024. The United Kingdom extended its 0% VAT rate on menstrual hygiene products (first introduced in January 2021) to include reusable period underwear from 1 January 2024, following a similar trend seen in numerous other jurisdictions. Azerbaijan introduced legislation providing for the refund of the VAT paid for medical services provided to foreigners and stateless persons by medical institutions and individuals engaged in private medical practice with a view to support the development of the medical sector.

Reduced VAT rates were also used to support the tourism sector and related businesses such as restaurants. In January 2024, Greece extended until June 30, 2024, the application of the reduced rate of 13% to services provided by restaurants, coffee shops, and similar businesses, excluding nightclubs, except for the supply of certain beverages. Peru extended the temporary reduction of the VAT rate from 18% to 10% on restaurant and hotel services provided by small and medium-sized enterprises. The measure, initially implemented in 2022, has been extended until December 2027. Uruguay extended, until 30 April 2025, the temporary application of the 9% reduced VAT rate introduced in 2023 for certain tourism-related activities, provided that payment is made by credit card, debit card, or electronic money. This initiative is intended to support the tourism sector while encouraging the use of electronic payment methods through financial incentives.

The agricultural sector remained a focus for VAT relief measures. Albania introduced a VAT exemption on the import of purebred live animals for reproduction, as well as biological materials used for artificial insemination, in order to boost livestock numbers and promote organic production. This exemption also applies to the import of beneficial insects and traps used to combat harmful pests, with the aim of developing the beekeeping sector, encouraging organic farming, and promoting innovation in agriculture. In Ireland, the flat-rate compensation for farmers (a special scheme for non-registered VAT farmers entitling them to a flat-rate refund on their agricultural outputs) was reduced from 5% to 4.8% in January 2024, and then increased to 5.1% in January 2025 in line with EU Directives. The flat-rate for farmers will also rise in Montenegro from 5% to 8% in January 2025. Mauritius introduced a 0% VAT on a set of agricultural goods including vegetables, fruits, flower seeds, plants, seedling trays, plant pots, and agricultural sprayers. Poland extended the application of an 8% VAT rate on a range of agricultural products such as soil improvers and fertilising materials. Portugal extended for the third time the temporary application of the 0% VAT rate on the supply of fertilisers, soil improvers, and animal feed for animals intended for human consumption, until 31 December 2025. In Uruguay, beekeepers and farmers of cattle, sheep, milk, rice, flowers, fruits, and vegetables, who are not subject to VAT, received a refund of the VAT paid on their gasoline purchases used in these activities. The VAT refunds took effect from 1 March 2024 for a period of one year and are subject to a maximum limit based on each producer's category and sales volume for the year.

Countries also continued to support the media and cultural sectors. Hungary extended the application of the reduced VAT rate of 18% to newspapers, and the 5% rate to works of art, in January 2024. Peru extended the VAT exemption on the import and supply of books, e-books, and related publishing products until the end of December 2025. Book publishers may request a VAT refund on inputs used in the production of such books, subject to approval by the National Library. In January 2025, Germany reduced its VAT rate on works of art and collectable items from 19% to 7%, reversing an increase introduced in 2014. Ireland further reduced its VAT rate on books and audiobooks from 9% to 0%.

Other sector-specific VAT rate reductions were implemented in Poland, Portugal and Türkiye. Poland reduced the VAT rate from 23% to 8% on certain beauty care and treatment services as of April 2024 to improve the financial conditions of entrepreneurs offering these services, including micro, small, and medium-sized enterprises. effective from January 2025, Portugal reduced its VAT rate on admission to bullfighting shows to 6%. Türkiye extended, until 31 December 2024, VAT relief for supplies made to taxpayers conducting research and development or other forms of innovation, as well as to certain manufacturing industry taxpayers. It also extended, until 31 December 2028, VAT relief for supplies made to projects related to education and health, urban rail transport systems, and for the delivery of immovable property to the social security institution.

Montenegro reformed its VAT legislation as part of its plan to align with EU VAT rules. The reform introduces a new 15% reduced VAT rate alongside the existing 7% rate, effective 1 January 2025. The standard 21% rate remains unchanged. Several supplies – such as accommodation, hospitality services, and books – were moved from the 7% to the new 15% rate, while the 7% rate continues to apply to essential goods and services such as basic foods, medicines, textbooks, animal food, and funeral services.

VAT incentives were also used to stimulate investment, support regional development, and promote domestic production. In Mexico, a package of tax incentives was introduced to attract investment in special industrial zones in the Yucatán Peninsula and Quintana Roo. These include a 100% VAT tax credit on the sale or temporary use of goods and services between taxpayers in these zones. Additional credits are available for individuals and corporations with lower turnover on the importation of goods, applicable from April 2024 to September 2030. Mexico also extended, until December 2025, the application of a 50% VAT credit – effectively reducing the rate to 8% – in its Northern and Southern border regions to stimulate growth and consumption. Similarly, Azerbaijan introduced VAT exemptions to support local production and develop its non-oil sector. These exemptions cover the sale of domestically manufactured buses and the import of their components, as well as the importation of machinery and technological equipment used in public-private partnership projects.

Increasingly, countries used reduced VAT rates and exemptions to promote environmental sustainability

Continuing a trend observed in recent years (OECD, 2024[7]), **several jurisdictions introduced or extended VAT rate reductions and exemptions for goods and services that support the transition to a low-carbon economy.** These measures often target energy-saving appliances, low-emission vehicles, and renewable energy equipment. In some cases, they are permanent; in others, they are designed as temporary incentives to encourage investment while allowing governments to assess the impact before committing to long-term revenue losses.

Numerous countries reduced VAT rates or applied exemptions to encourage renewable energy investments to private residences and other buildings. Ireland, for example, reduced the VAT rate on the supply and installation of heat pumps from 23% to 9%, effective January 2025. Furthermore, Ireland extended the 0% VAT rate on the supply and installation of solar panels for private dwellings to schools in January 2024. From January 2024 to December 2025, Austria applied a 0% VAT rate to the supply and installation of photovoltaic systems.[4] In Belgium, the reduced VAT rate of 6% for the supply and installation of solar panels and heat pumps, introduced in 2022 as a temporary measure, ended for solar panels in December 2023 as planned but was extended until the end of 2024 for heat pump installations. Portugal introduced a 6% VAT rate for the supply, installation, and repair of equipment used primarily for collecting and using solar, wind, geothermal, and other renewable energy. The United Kingdom extended the 0% VAT rate on the supply and installation of energy-saving appliances in residential buildings in place until 2027, to include buildings used solely for relevant charitable purposes and a wider range of technologies.

Electric and low-emission vehicles remained a key focus of VAT relief measures. Iceland extended its VAT exemption on the sale of used electric, hydrogen, and plug-in hybrid vehicles for two more years (2024–2025), subject to a cap. Additionally, it also extended the temporary reduced 5% VAT rate for the supply of bicycles and green motorbikes, subject to a cap, through the end of 2024. Barbados prolonged its VAT exemption for the purchase of electric vehicles until March 2026. Korea extended its temporary VAT rebate for the purchase of hybrid and electric vehicles until the end of 2026.

Nigeria and Azerbaijan introduced VAT exemptions aimed at supporting broader clean energy infrastructure and production. In Nigeria, changes to the tax code from 1 September 2024 included VAT exemptions for equipment and infrastructure related to Compressed Natural Gas (CNG) and Liquefied Petroleum Gas (LPG) expansion, domestic LNG processing facilities, electric vehicles and their components, and biogas and biofuel equipment used for clean cooking and transport. Similarly, Azerbaijan introduced a VAT exemption for producers of electricity from renewable energy sources, applicable for the duration of agreements with state and municipal authorities under electricity purchase contracts.

Conversely, some VAT rate increases were used to remove preferential treatment for activities not aligned with environmental objectives. In Italy, for example, the reduced VAT rate was restricted by increasing it from the 10% reduced rate to the 22% standard rate for waste disposal activities not consistent with circular economy principles, such as landfilling and incineration without energy recovery.

Jurisdictions also used reduced VAT rates as support measures in response to natural disasters

In 2024, VAT relief measures continued to be applied in response to natural disasters. Temporary VAT relief introduced in Mexico in October 2023 for zones affected by Hurricane Otis was extended until February 2024. In Poland, from 12 September to 31 December 2024, donations of goods and services provided to assist victims of the September 2024 flooding were subject to a temporary 0% VAT rate when made to public benefit organisations, local government units, medical entities, or the Agency of Strategic Reserves. The 0% VAT rate also applied, from 24 September 2024 until 31 March 2025, to donations of construction materials transferred directly to natural persons, as well as to entities engaged in educational and cultural activities, healthcare, childcare, elderly care, collective accommodation for pupils and students, and organisational units or other entities involved in social assistance, whose real estate was damaged by the flooding. Türkiye extended the VAT relief for the supply of goods and services made to professional organisations for the constructions of dwellings donated to the victims of the earthquakes until 31 December 2024. A new temporary VAT relief was introduced in August 2024 until end December 2025 for the supply of goods and services in relation to immovable properties built for donating to public administrations.

On the other hand, temporary VAT zero-rates and exemptions on products used to mitigate the COVID-19 pandemic have been almost universally withdrawn. Canada, for example, repealed the temporary GST/HST relief on supplies of certain face masks, respirators, and face shields in July 2024.

Some countries extended temporary VAT cuts introduced in 2022 and 2023 in response to rising price levels

Temporary application of reduced VAT rates was viewed by a number of governments as a quick way to counter rising prices in sectors considered essential for the population. In Canada, as part of the national strategy to address the surge in housing prices, the government temporarily increased the federal portion of the GST/HST rebate from 36% to 100% and removed the existing GST rebate phase-out thresholds for the construction of new rental housing projects. This measure, applicable to constructions that begin after 13 September 2023 and before 2031, aims to encourage the development of affordable rental housing across the country. The measure was also extended to not-for-profit universities, public colleges, and school authorities in respect of new student housing. The governments of Ontario, New Brunswick, Nova Scotia, Prince Edward Island, and Newfoundland and Labrador have mirrored the federal 100% rebate on the provincial portion of the HST in those provinces. The government of Saskatchewan had previously introduced a 42% rebate on the Provincial Sales Tax (as it does not apply the HST) for the purchase of newly constructed homes after 1 April 2023 and occupied before 1 April 2026. In Greece, the temporary VAT suspension regime introduced in 2020 has been extended until 31 December 2025. Under this regime, the supply of newly built property is not subject to VAT, while real estate builders are not permitted to deduct input VAT. In Croatia, the temporary reduction of the VAT rate from 13% to 5% on natural gas and heating, fuel wood, pellets, briquettes, and wood chips – introduced in 2023 – was extended until the end of March 2026. In Ireland, the temporary reduced rate of 9% for the supply of gas and electricity, introduced in 2022, was extended again until 30 April 2025. Barbados further extended, until 30 September 2024, the application of the reduced VAT rate of 7.5% (instead of 17.5%) on the first 250 kWh of electricity per month for residential properties.

An increasing number of countries, however, began phasing out temporary rate cuts introduced during periods of high inflation

A number of jurisdictions scaled back their temporary reduced rates in 2024 as inflationary pressures continued to ease. On 31 December 2024, Bulgaria ended the temporary application of the 0% VAT rate on bread and flour introduced in 2022, reverting to the standard rate of 20%. It also ended the reduced VAT rate of 9% for the supply of certain touristic services and the use of sports facilities in June 2024, and for restaurant and catering services in December 2024. In Germany, the reduced VAT rate on gas and district heating, which had been lowered to 7% in October 2022, returned to the standard rate of 19% in April 2024. Poland, which had extended the temporary 0% VAT rate on basic food introduced in 2022, ended the measure on 31 March 2024, with these products reverting to the reduced rate of 5%. The Spanish government, which introduced temporary VAT rate reductions in 2022, ended the 0% VAT rate on basic foodstuffs, gradually returning them to the 4% reduced rate, with an interim increase to 2% on 1 October 2024 and to 4% in January 2025. The VAT rate on seed oil and pasta, which was reduced from 10% to 5% in July 2024, was increased to 7.5% until 31 December 2024. By contrast, the VAT rate on olive oil and fermented milk was reduced from 10% to 4%. The VAT rate on electricity, which had been temporarily reduced from 21% to 5%, was increased to 10% on 1 January 2024 while the temporary 5% reduced rate on natural gas and briquettes, pellets and firewood respectively ended on 31 March and 30 June 2024.

Some jurisdictions also raised their VAT rate on specific areas of the economy

While several countries have implemented reduced VAT rates to support environmental, economic, or social goals, others have increased VAT rates on certain sectors or goods and services, primarily to raise additional revenue or simplify their VAT systems. In Estonia, the reduced VAT rate on accommodation services was increased from 9% to 13%, and on newspaper and magazine publications, including electronic editions, from 5% to 9%, effective January 2025. In Finland, from 1 January 2025, goods and services previously subject to a reduced VAT rate of 10% – including books, pharmaceutical products, physical exercise services, passenger transport, and accommodation – are now taxed at a rate of 14%. However, public broadcasting, newspapers, and periodicals remain subject to the 10% rate. The Slovak Republic abolished the 10% reduced VAT rate on alcoholic beverages served in restaurants, applying the standard rate of 20% from January 2024. To both increase revenues and discourage the consumption of unhealthy drinks, Slovenia raised its VAT rate on sugary and flavoured beverages from 9.5% to 22% on 1 January 2025. Türkiye increased the VAT rate on certain foods for special medical purposes from 1% to 10%, and the rate on medical devices from 10% to the standard rate of 20% in November 2024. Türkiye also abolished the VAT exemption for services provided to transport vehicles used for activities such as sightseeing, sports, and fishing, effective from September 2024. Switzerland adjusted its reduced VAT rate from 3.7 to 3.8% as of 1 January 2024 as part of the VAT rate increases intended to fund social security expenditures.

3.4.3. Eight countries increased their standard VAT rates in an acceleration of a trend that emerged in 2023

To mobilise revenues, five countries increased their standard VAT rates in 2024. Estonia raised its rate from 20% to 22% in January 2024 to help rebalance the general budget, with a further increase to 24% planned for July 2025. Singapore continued its progressive VAT increase, raising the standard rate from 8% to 9% on 1 January 2024, following a previous increase from 7% to 8% in January 2023. Finland increased its standard VAT rate from 24% to 25.5% in September 2024, and Switzerland raised its rate from 7.7% to 8.1% on 1 January 2024. In Luxembourg, the standard VAT rate returned to 17% in January 2024, following a temporary 12-month reduction to 16% aimed at mitigating inflationary pressures.

Three additional countries increased their standard VAT rates effective from January 2025. Indonesia raised its standard rate from 11% to 12%, However, to compensate the impact of this rate increase on consumer prices, the base on which the VAT amount is calculated is reduced to eleven-twelfths of the value of the supply, resulting in an effective VAT rate of 11%. Israel increased its standard VAT rate from 17% to 18%, while the Slovak Republic raised its rate from 20% to 23%.

3.4.4. VAT base adjustments were predominately used to strengthen revenues and modernise the VAT system

Jurisdictions continued to adapt their VAT systems to the digitalisation of the economy

In 2024, several countries updated their VAT legislation to improve VAT collection on digital trade. In Greece, effective 1 January 2024, legal entities renting one or more properties and individuals renting more than two properties for short-term accommodation (e.g. via digital platforms) are now subject to the VAT rate of 13%. Landlords renting fewer than three properties remain VAT-exempt. Japan will implement a "Platform Taxation" regime in April 2025, requiring digital platforms, where transaction value under the regime exceed JPY 5 billion (about EUR 30 million) per taxable period, to collect and remit VAT on inbound digital supplies. Peru introduced new legislation, effective 1 December 2024, requiring non-resident suppliers of digital services to register for, collect, and remit the 18% standard VAT on cross-border supplies to final consumers in Peru. These rules reflect the OECD's *International VAT/GST* Guidelines. This new regime also includes a VAT withholding mechanism where payment service providers (e.g. credit card companies) must withhold VAT if non-resident suppliers fail to register, file returns, pay VAT, or submit required declarations. This withholding mechanism, however, does not exempt non-compliant suppliers from their VAT obligations or potential penalties. As part of its preparation for the EU accession process, North Macedonia imposed, effective 1 January 2024, VAT registration and compliance requirements on non-resident suppliers of digital and telecommunications services to final consumers, including the appointment of a fiscal representative.

While most of these reforms to date have been aimed at the collection of VAT on online sales of digital services and products, countries are increasingly considering further reform to ensure that VAT is also collected effectively on online sales of low-value imported goods. To date, 41 jurisdictions have implemented such reforms. In Chile, Congress approved a bill (see Box 3.3) applying VAT to low-value shipments of goods imported directly to consumers, effective October 2025. Any consignment valued at or below USD 500 will be subject to VAT at the point of sale, with sellers required to register, collect, and remit VAT under a simplified registration scheme. There is no registration threshold. If a seller fails to register, payment service providers (e.g. credit card companies) will be required to withhold VAT. Montenegro, as part of its progressive harmonisation of its VAT regime with that of the European Union (of which it is a candidate for accession) has abolished its VAT exemption threshold for imported products of EUR 75.

Box 3.6. International VAT/GST Guidelines

VAT reforms to address the challenges of an increasingly digitalised economy continue to be among the most impactful changes made by jurisdictions to VAT policy and its administration. To address the transformation of economies through globalisation and digitalisation, the OECD has delivered a set of internationally agreed upon standards and recommended approaches for the VAT treatment of international trade, with a particular focus on digital trade. These include the International VAT/GST Guidelines (OECD, 2017[10]) as well as a series of implementation guidance documents. To date, over 100 jurisdictions worldwide – including many low- and middle-income economies – have implemented reforms based on these VAT standards and subsequent implementation guidance, with a further 25 jurisdictions in the process of implementing or considering doing so.

A set of jurisdictions also introduced targeted VAT base broadening measures

To broaden their VAT bases, several countries have recently revised VAT rules on specific goods and services. Austria abolished the VAT exemption for services provided between banks, insurance companies, and pension funds. In January 2025, the United Kingdom removed the VAT exemption for education and vocational training services provided by private schools, making them subject to the standard VAT rate of 20%.

A few jurisdictions implemented policy measures to selectively narrow the VAT base by exempting specific goods and services from VAT

A limited number of jurisdictions introduced policy measures that selectively narrow their VAT base by exempting specific goods and services. Germany extended the VAT exemption for the management of certain funds. All alternative investment funds – including private equity, venture capital, real estate, infrastructure, and crypto funds – are now covered by the VAT exemption. Mauritius introduced a VAT exemption on the construction of purpose-built educational facilities to include pre-primary and technical education, with retrospective effect from September 2023. It also exempted the importation and supply of motor vehicles linked to construction activities, for approved contractors engaged in social housing projects under contracts with the New Social Living Development, with retrospective effect from August 2023. The United Arab Emirates extended VAT exemptions to include investment fund management services, virtual assets, and digital currencies, as part of its efforts to simplify its VAT system.

Ten countries increased their VAT registration thresholds to support small enterprises

To ease compliance costs for small suppliers and reduce administrative burdens on tax authorities, several countries increased their VAT registration thresholds. Since 2022, two countries have implemented phased increases to their thresholds. Portugal, following a phased increase, raised its threshold from EUR 13 500 in January 2023 to EUR 14 500 in January 2024 and to EUR 15 000 in January 2025. Sweden increased its threshold from SEK 80 000 (EUR 7 000) to SEK 120 000 (EUR 11 000) in January 2025, following a previous increase from SEK 30 000 to SEK 80 000 in 2022. In 2024, four countries increased their thresholds: Ireland raised its thresholds from EUR 75 000 to EUR 80 000 for goods and from EUR 37 500 to EUR 40 000 for services in January 2024; Latvia increased its threshold from EUR 40 000 to EUR 50 000 in January 2024, Namibia increased its threshold from NAD 500 000 (EUR 24 000) to NAD 1 million (EUR 48 000) in November 2024, and the United Kingdom raised its threshold from GBP 85 000 to GBP 90 000 in April 2024. Effective from January 2025, Croatia, Finland, and Slovenia also raised their thresholds – from EUR 40 000 to EUR 60 000, EUR 15 000 to EUR 20 000, and EUR 50 000 to EUR 60 000 respectively.

Box 3.7. Jurisdictions continue to take measures to prevent and combat VAT Fraud and non-compliance

Given the significance of VAT as a key revenue source for governments globally, the revenues at risk from VAT fraud and non-compliance can often be considerable. Reducing the vulnerability of VAT regimes to VAT fraud and non-compliance and limiting the associated revenue losses therefore remain key priorities for governments, and the growth of online trade has exacerbated these risks. On the other hand, digitalisation also offers significant opportunity for tax administrations to enhance the capacity and efficiency of their detection, prevention and treatment strategies, notably by giving them significantly greater access to relevant data and greater analytical capacity to use them effectively.

As part of this strategy, governments increasingly use technology to enhance the reporting of relevant data to tax authorities. after the general implementation of mandatory e-filing of VAT returns, many jurisdictions have introduced or consider introducing a requirement for taxpayers to make transactional data available to tax authorities, sometimes in (near) real time. These measures, which present considerable variety in design and operation across countries, are typically aimed at enhancing tax administrations' VAT compliance risk management strategies and their VAT enforcement capacity. This information at the individual taxable transaction level can include invoicing information and accounting data or any other information that allows tax authorities to monitor supplies made and/or received by individual taxpayers and determine their tax liability. In OECD countries, there has been a gradual shift from paper invoices to electronic invoices, the latter now being permitted in all of them and even mandatory for business-to-business (B2B) supplies in 7 of these countries (OECD, 2024[9]). In its "VAT in Digital Age" (ViDA) proposal, the European Commission proposes to make electronic invoicing the norm in all Member States as of 1 January 2030. Among the surveyed countries for this report, the United Arab Emirates indicated that electronic invoicing was now recognised by its tax administration and Poland announced its intention to make it mandatory for B2B supplies soon.

Payment data is also increasingly being used by tax authorities as part of their compliance strategies. Within the European Union as of 1 January 2024, new transparency rules require payment service providers (PSPs) offering services in the EU to monitor the beneficiaries of cross-border payments. The information collected is stored in the Central Electronic System of Payment information (CESOP) and made available to Member States' anti-fraud experts via the EU network of liaison officials from the 27 Member States and Norway set up to combat cross-border VAT fraud (Eurofisc).

International administrative cooperation is also critical for the effective management of international VAT risks. Governments increasingly recognise that information exchange and other forms of administrative co-operation play a critical role in tax administrations' strategies to ensure the effective collection of VAT and to tackle VAT fraud and non-compliance, not least in the context of the digitalisation of the economy and fast-growing digital trade.

A number of instruments are available that provide a legal foundation for the international administrative co-operation in VAT matters. These include the Multilateral Convention on Mutual Administrative Assistance in Tax Matters, the bilateral treaties implementing Articles 26 and 27 of the OECD and UN Model Tax Conventions; and Tax Information Exchange Agreements (TIEAs) based on the OECD Model. Regional agreements can also provide a legal base for such co-operation.

3.4.5. Countries further raised health taxes to raise revenues and discourage behaviours that adversely affect both individual and public health

Health-related taxes are most commonly implemented through excise duties, which differ from broad-based goods and services taxes in that they apply only to specific products. The excise taxes may be applied to the harmful ingredient itself – such as alcohol content, sugar, salt, or saturated fat – or to the final product that contains it, like a litre of soft drink, an alcoholic beverage, or a pack of cigarettes (OECD, 2024[11]). In 27 of the 38 OECD countries, revenues from excise taxes on tobacco were the principal source of health tax revenues (OECD, 2024[12]).

Sixteen countries implemented or announced increases to their tax burden on tobacco products to improve public health and raise tobacco tax revenues (Armenia, Australia, Bulgaria, Canada, Estonia, Finland, Georgia, Hungary, Iceland, Ireland, Lithuania, Poland, the Slovak Republic, Slovenia, Spain, the United Kingdom). In many of those countries increases to excise taxes on tobacco included new or expanded taxes on vaping products or nicotine pouches. Iceland, Ireland, Poland, and Spain, for example, all introduced new or expanded excise taxes on e-cigarettes and their associated liquids. The United Kingdom announced the introduction of a Vaping Products Duty (VPD) starting in October 2026, alongside a one-off tobacco duty increase to maintain price incentives for switching from smoking to vaping. In Canada, nine out of thirteen provinces/territories have signed the Coordinated Vaping Product Agreement with the federal government and have implemented the coordinated vaping product system, which would double the excise duties on vaping products sold in those jurisdicitons. Additionally, Alberta and Quebec increased their excise taxes on tobacco products (including smokeless tobacco in Alberta).

Countries also raised their existing excise taxes on all tobacco related products. Bulgaria, for instance, introduced a comprehensive five-year plan (2025 – 2029) to raise excise duties on all tobacco products, including cigarettes, cigars, heated tobacco, e-cigarette liquids, and tobacco substitutes such as nicotine pouches. Slovenia increased excise duty on all tobacco products, with the highest increase for heated tobacco and e-cigarettes. Estonia continued its annual 5% increases in tobacco excise taxes through 2028 to discourage tobacco consumption, increase tax revenues, and ensure tobacco products do not become more affordable as price levels and incomes increase. Finland scheduled six increases to its tobacco tax between late 2024 and mid-2027. Lithuania increased its excise taxes on tobacco products and e-cigarette liquids. Australia implemented a planned 5% annual increase of its tobacco excise tax, noted in the previous edition of this report. Georgia increased excise duties on various tobacco and nicotine products, including cigarettes, cigars, cigarillos, and inhalation products. At the same time, it reduced excise rates on raw and certain smokeless tobacco products to support local producers and curb the illegal cigarette trade.

Seven countries raised excise duties on alcohol products, including Armenia, Estonia, Finland, Lithuania, Montenegro, Netherlands, South Africa, United Kingdom. Estonia scheduled multiple alcohol excise increases, including a 10% increase of its excise tax on alcohol products from 2026 and a further 5% increase in 2027 and 2028. Finland introduced a multi-year increase in alcohol taxes on strong alcoholic beverages from 2025 to 2027, in order to adjust the excise tax level to inflation. Lithuania increased excise duties on alcoholic beverages in an effort to shift the tax burden toward health-related taxes and align with international recommendations on growth-friendly tax policy.

The United Kingdom and Montenegro both increased their alcohol taxes while also introducing targeted reductions to support local businesses. The United Kingdom increased excise taxes on bottled or canned alcoholic beverages in line with inflation, while slightly reducing taxes on eligible draught products below an alcohol level of 8.5%. Similarly, Montenegro increased its excise tax on wines, while introducing a reduced rate for small wine producers to support the economic development of the sector.

At least two countries expanded or adjusted taxes on Sugar Sweetened Beverages (SSBs). The Estonia introduced a new tax on SSBs in general and the United Kingdom indexed its excise tax on soft drinks to inflation and also implemented additional increases over the next 5 years to catch up with cumulative inflation lost since 2018, ensuring the tax remains effective.

A few targeted reductions were introduced to support economic or behavioural policy goals. New Zealand made permanent a 50% reduction to its excise duty on heated tobacco products, aiming to support smokers switching away from cigarettes. Sweden reduced alcohol excise duties for small independent breweries to support small businesses and investment.

3.5. Environmentally related taxes

Over the past decade, environmental sustainability has become an increasingly important aspect of tax policy design. Some taxes classified as environmentally related in this section, such as carbon taxes, air pollution taxes, or plastic taxes, have been designed explicitly to disincentivize a negative externality related to the environment. Such taxes aim to incorporate price signals into consumer decisions, thereby applying the polluter-pays principle to encourage greener economic activities and consumption choices. Some other taxes were initially implemented as a source of revenue, such as vehicle taxes, fuel excise taxes or air ticket taxes, but are implicitly acting as environmental taxes as they increase the price of an environmentally damaging activity or good. Finally, taxes such as CIT, PIT, and VAT are increasingly incorporating environmental considerations to incentivize the uptake and the use of clean technologies. Environmentally related incentives for these taxes are discussed in the respective sections.

Environmentally related taxes are applied to tax bases considered to have significant environmental relevance, such as energy, vehicles, waste, water, emissions, or resource extraction. In some cases, there is a direct link between the tax base and the environmental externality. For example, a tax rate might be defined per gramme of CO_2 emitted per kilometer driven, per tonne of pollutant released, or per tonne of plastic recycled. In other cases, the connection is less direct and based on proxies, such as using travel distance as a basis for air ticket taxes.

A notable shift from previous years is that several countries have planned gradual increases in fuel excise taxes with the objective of boosting their revenue. In 2022 and 2023, policymakers implemented temporary cuts to excise taxes on road transport fuels and residential electricity consumption to alleviate cost-of-living pressures. As of 2024, fuel excise tax rates have started to rise again, following a predetermined upward trajectory set to continue over the coming years.

For the second consecutive year, several high-income countries have strengthened explicit carbon pricing to support the transition to a low-carbon economy. Several countries with existing carbon taxes implemented significant rate increases, while others expanded their tax base by introducing new carbon taxes and extending taxation to additional sectors, such as international shipping and agriculture.

As in the previous year, several countries raised vehicle taxes to increase revenue while maintaining a relative advantage for low-carbon vehicles. Revenue mobilisation has resulted in higher vehicle tax rates. Full exemptions for electric vehicles (EVs) continued to be phased out by governments. The relative tax advantage of EVs, however, was often maintained or even reinforced in countries implementing vehicle tax rate increases on an emissions-based tax structure.

Few changes were made to other environmental tax bases, which still hold potential for both revenue generation and environmental benefits. Aviation taxes were strengthened in three European countries, with one adopting a tax structure more closely linked to emissions. Tourist taxes continued to expand in two countries. However, other environmentally related taxes, such as those on pollution and waste, remained largely unchanged in 2024.

3.5.1. Recent trends in carbon pricing

According to OECD research, in 2023 79% of the GHG emissions remained unpriced in the 79 countries for which the OECD calculates effective carbon rates (ECRs), a share similar to past years. The share of emissions with a positive price is expected to increase slightly in 2024 as governments phase out temporary measures linked to the energy crisis, as well as in the coming years with the implementation of the planned expansion of carbon pricing schemes outside traditional sectors (e.g. agriculture, maritime shipping).

The distribution of ECRs is currently heterogenous across sectors, with the road transport sector facing rates at least four times higher than other sectors. However, countries' responses to the energy crisis have brought about a significant reduction in the Net ECR of buildings, road transport and agriculture, while marginally higher explicit carbon prices increased the Net ECR of industry and electricity. Variations in average price levels across sectors can be attributed to the differences in the pricing instruments employed to account for their emissions, the extent of coverage, and the variance in fuel usage among sectors. ECRs were notably higher in sectors primarily covered by fuel excise taxes, particularly in road transport. Conversely, lower ECRs are found in sectors mainly covered by emissions trading systems (ETSs), such as the electricity and industry sectors.

Figure 3.6. Average effective carbon prices and GHG emissions by sector, 2021-2023

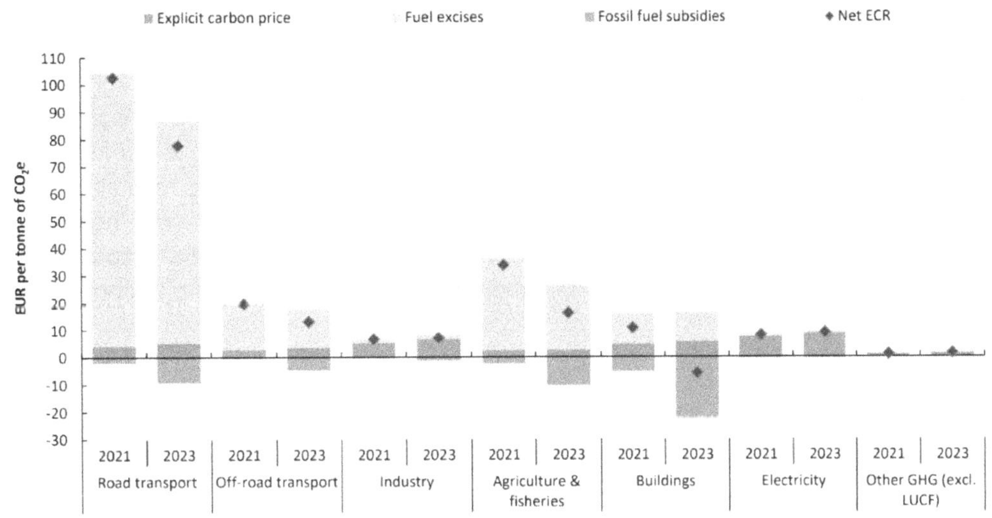

Note: Effective carbon rates are averaged across all GHG emissions of the 79 countries, including those emissions that are not covered by any carbon pricing instrument. Due to data limitations, fossil fuel subsidy estimates for 2023 are based on data for 2022. All rates are expressed in real 2023 EUR using the latest available OECD exchange rate and inflation data; changes can thus be affected by inflation and exchange rate fluctuations. Prices are rounded to the nearest eurocent. GHG emissions are the sum of fossil-fuel related CO2 emissions, calculated based on energy use data for 2021 from the IEA World Energy Balance and other GHGs from Climate Watch.
Source: (OECD, 2022[13])

3.5.2. Carbon taxes increased both in terms of their rate and base, alongside fuel excise taxes also beginning to rise again

Following the trend initiated in 2023, countries further strengthened carbon taxes, with significant rate increases in several countries. In 2025, Iceland raised its carbon tax rate by 59%, though this was lower than the initially proposed 100% increase. Ireland will increase its carbon tax rate from EUR 56 to EUR 63.50 per tonne of CO_2e, while in Slovenia, the CO_2 tax rose by 80% in September 2024. South Africa increased its carbon tax from ZAR 159 to ZAR 190 per tonne of CO_2 e as of January 1, 2024. In

Norway, carbon taxes on emissions from non-ETS sectors and the offshore petroleum industry increased by 16%.

In addition to rate increases, carbon tax coverage is expanding, with several countries planning to extend carbon pricing to new sectors. Lithuania will introduce a CO_2 component to fuel excise taxes, while Denmark announced a carbon tax on agriculture, set to be applied to greenhouse gas emissions from agricultural lime and livestock from 2030 (see Box 3.8). As part of this reform, Denmark will also increase and harmonise duties on F-gases. Norway has decided to introduce a reduced CO_2 tax on mineral products for international shipping at NOK 500 per tonne of CO_2, though its implementation depends on compliance with state aid regulations (see Box 3.9 for more information on shipping). Norway also expanded its carbon tax base to include emissions from distant offshore fishing.

Box 3.8. The Danish carbon tax on agriculture

In 2021, non-energy-related emissions from agriculture and forestry accounted for 27% of Denmark's total greenhouse gas (GHG) emissions, including approximately 80% of the country's methane and nitrous oxide emissions (Expert Group for Green Tax Reform, 2022[14]). To address this, policymakers have introduced a carbon pricing scheme aimed at reducing CO_2e emissions in these sectors by 30% by 2030.

Implementation process

To develop the carbon pricing framework, the government appointed an expert group to provide recommendations, which were then discussed with stakeholders, including the agricultural sector, climate organisations, and other interest groups. In June 2024, the Green Tripartite Agreement established a carbon pricing scheme for GHG emissions in agriculture. By November 2024, a political agreement was reached on the implementation of the scheme based on these recommendations. The agreement was, among other reasons, reached by combining the carbon tax with revenue recycling through subsidies for farmers. The tax administration will oversee implementation by calculating emissions using verified activity data - primarily manure and livestock accounts reported by farmers - combined with emissions factors.

Effective carbon prices

The effective carbon tax will be set at EUR 40 per tonne of CO_2e for livestock emissions and EUR 100 per tonne of CO_2e for agricultural lime emissions. To support the transition, tax revenues will be reinvested into subsidies, including for carbon-rich low-lying soils (EUR 5 per tonne of CO_2e), reduction in fertilizer applied to fields (EUR 100 per tonne of CO_2e) and afforestation (EUR 60 per tonne of CO_2e).

To raise revenue, multiple countries have scheduled fuel excise tax increases starting from 2025. Estonia will implement an annual 5% increase in the gasoline tax rate from 2025 to 2028, following a period of no change since 2018. New Zealand plans annual increases in fuel excise duties on motor gasoline and road user charges on diesel, starting in 2027. Latvia has raised excise duties on fuel, natural gas, and petroleum gases used for heating in 2025, while Lithuania has introduced small increases in excise rates on diesel, coal, and coke products, alongside a new carbon tax component as part of its green tax reform. In Israel, fuel excise tax reforms aim to better reflect carbon pricing. Over six years, starting in 2025, excise tax rates on coal, LPG, fuel oil, petroleum coke, and natural gas will gradually increase, reaching approximately EUR 55 per tonne of CO_2e by 2030. Conversely, Sweden will reduce fuel excise taxes on gasoline and diesel.

Exemptions and reduced rates related to fuel excise duties remained overall unchanged. However, Latvia abolished the excise duty exemption for petroleum products used in electricity generation and cogeneration.

Several countries have adjusted taxation in the agriculture and forestry sectors, which traditionally benefit from reduced rates, refunds, or exemptions. In the Netherlands, the CO_2 tax for greenhouse horticulture will be phased in more gradually than initially planned. Sweden will continue to apply reduced fuel excise rates for agriculture, forestry, and aquaculture, while Germany is phasing out diesel tax refunds for agriculture and forestry from 2024 to 2026.

Hydrogen and electricity rates were changed in only one country. The Netherlands will introduce a reduced tax rate for hydrogen from 2026, setting it lower than the rate for natural gas, which is currently taxed at the same level. This reduced rate is expected to remain in place beyond 2030 to encourage investment. Additionally, the Netherlands increased the Electricity Industry Levy, while Sweden withdrew a proposal to introduce a reduced tax rate for electricity used in carbon capture and storage (CCS).

Subsidies for renewable energy generation prompted tax policy adjustments in two countries. In South Africa, the government increased the eligibility threshold for renewable energy projects under the Embedded Generation Initiative from 15 megawatts to 30 megawatts to offset allowances for the carbon tax. Meanwhile, in the Netherlands, the net metering scheme for small-scale solar panel users will be phased out starting in 2027, which will result in higher electricity excise tax revenues.

Table 3.10. Changes to taxes related to energy use and emissions

	Rate decrease/Base narrowing	Rate increase/Base broadening
Fuel excise tax - generic	SWE	ISR, LTU
Fuel excise tax - other	NLD	
Fuel excise tax – agriculture and forestry	IRL	DEU
Fuel excise tax – energy industries		
Fuel excise tax - transport	NZL	DNK[diesel], NZL
Fuel excise tax - industry		NLD, LVA
Electricity and hydrogen excise tax	NLD	NLD[RE], NZL, SWE, ZAF[RE]
Carbon tax	NLD	DNK, IRL, ISL, LTU, NLD, NOR, SVN, ZAF
ETS		

Note: diesel denotes a measure related to diesel fuel, RE to renewable energy.
Source: Tax Policy Reform questionnaire.

Box 3.9. The pricing of emissions from international shipping

International maritime transport is responsible for 3% of global greenhouse gas (GHG) emissions but remained largely exempt from climate-related regulations until recently. At present, no fuel excise tax, carbon tax, or emissions trading system (ETS) applies to fuel consumption or emissions in this sector. However, several regional and international initiatives have been agreed on with the aim to introduce carbon pricing mechanisms and regulations in the coming years.

Negotiations over carbon pricing for global shipping

The International Maritime Organization (IMO) is leading discussions on global regulations for the shipping industry. The 2023 IMO Strategy outlined a plan to transition toward low-emission fuels and renewable energy and achieve net-zero emissions in maritime transport by 2050. It also sets interim targets of reducing emissions by at least 20% by 2030 and 70% by 2040, relative to 2008 levels (IMO, 2023[15]).

In April 2025, the Marine Environment Protection Committee approved draft regulations for an IMO net-zero framework. The regulations would introduce a new fuel standard for ships and a carbon pricing mechanism for emissions that exceed the established targets. The fuel standard is set to include two greenhouse gas fuel intensity (GFI) reduction targets: a base target and a direct compliance target. Targets are based on the full lifecycle GHG emissions of shipping fuel and are set to be progressively tightened starting in 2028.

The global carbon pricing mechanism would take the form of a fine per tonne of CO_2e emitted above the GFI targets. For the 2028 – 2030 reporting period, the price is set at USD 100 per tonne for emissions that fall between the base and direct compliance targets, and USD 380 per tonne for emissions exceeding the base target. This system is expected to generate an estimated USD 11-13 billion annually. The revenue will be used to support innovation and mitigate negative impacts on vulnerable states.

The agreement still needs to be formally adopted in October 2025 and is set to enter into force in 2028 for all large ships (above 5 000 gross tonnage).

Regional carbon pricing initiative in the EU

Since 2024, the European Union's Emissions Trading System (EU ETS) include GHG emissions from all large ships (above 5 000 gross tonnage) (European Commission, 2025[16]). The system applies to: (i) 50% of emissions from voyages that start or end outside the EU, (ii) 100% of emissions from voyages between EU ports and those generated while ships are within EU ports. To facilitate a gradual transition, shipping companies will only be required to surrender allowances for a portion of their emissions during the phase-in period, from 40% of verified emissions in 2025 to 100% in 2027.

3.5.3. Revenue raising and environmental objectives drove transport-related tax reforms

Reforms in vehicle taxation across several countries were motivated by both revenue generation and environmental policy goals. Latvia increased vehicle operation tax rates by 10% for all vehicles, while Hungary raised the motor vehicle tax. Additionally, both Hungary and Latvia implemented significant increases in company car taxes, with hikes of 20% starting in 2025 and 10% starting in 2027 respectively. South Africa increased its motor vehicle emissions tax for passenger cars, and Armenia raised environmental tax rates.

In some countries, trade-offs between different vehicle taxes were made to limit the overall tax burden on drivers. Denmark increased the diesel excise tax while proportionally lowering the recurrent vehicle tax on diesel cars and the road use tax for trucks. Slovakia reduced car taxes for freight transport vehicles as part of a broader initiative that included higher highway tolls and lower car taxes for selected vehicle categories.

A number of countries are adjusting vehicle taxation for electric vehicles (EVs) as the transition to a greener fleet progresses. The Netherlands will phase out the motor vehicle tax exemption for emission-free passenger cars: it announced that a 40% reduction of the tax will be introduced in 2026, which will gradually decrease until in 2031. Other emission-free vehicles, including buses, will lose their tax discount starting in 2026. In Finland, where fleet electrification is already well underway, the government increased vehicle taxation on EVs and plug-in hybrids (PHEVs) by raising the basic tax and the tax on driving power for these vehicles. Hungary abolished the motor vehicle tax exemption for hybrid cars, maintaining tax benefits exclusively for fully electric vehicles. Meanwhile, New Zealand did not renew the Road User Charge (RUC) exemption for EVs, meaning that, as of April 2024, battery electric vehicles (BEVs) are taxed at NZD 76 per 1 000 kilometers, and PHEVs at NZD 38 per 1 000 kilometers. Conversely, Ireland introduced an emissions-based approach to its Vehicle Registration Tax for commercial vehicles in July 2025, with a lower 8% rate for vehicles with CO_2 emissions of less than 120 grams per kilometer.

There were few reforms aimed at transitioning to road use taxation. Lithuania is moving from a vignette-based system to an electronic tolling system for trucks, where charges are based on the number of kilometres driven.

A couple of European countries are increasing aviation taxes, with one strengthening the link to environmental externalities. Germany raised aviation tax rates, while the Netherlands will introduce distance-based differentiation in its aviation tax, taxing long-haul flights at higher rates. To adjust its Air Passenger Duty (APD) to the inflation of ticket prices, the United Kingdom has scheduled an increase inAPD, starting with higher rates on non-economy flights in 2025, followed by increases across all fare categories in 2026-27. Additionally, the APD for larger private jets will increase by 50%, and from 2027-28, rates will be rounded to the nearest penny. Conversely, Sweden abolished its air travel tax, marking a divergence from the broader trend of increasing aviation-related levies.

Table 3.11. Changes to taxes related to transport

	Rate decrease/Base narrowing	Rate decrease/Base narrowing
One-off vehicle tax	IRL[EV]	ARM
Recurrent vehicle tax	DNK, SVK, SWE	CAN[EV], DNK, FIN[EV], HUN[EV], HUN, LVA, NLD[EV,AF], ZAF
Road use ta	DNK	NZL[EV]
Air ticket tax	SWE	DEU, GBR, NLD

Note: EV denotes a measure related to electric vehicles, AF to alternative fuels.
Source: Tax Policy Reform questionnaire.

3.5.4. Tourism taxes continued to expand, while other environmentally related taxes were subject to little changes

Tourism-related taxes continued to expand, driven by both environmental and revenue-raising objectives. Greece increased rates for the climate crisis resiliency charge, while Iceland introduced a new infrastructure fee for tourists arriving on international cruise ships and raised the overnight tax rate. In contrast, Turks and Caicos implemented a waiver on penalties and interest for outstanding Hotel, Restaurant, and Tourism Tax payments starting in March 2024.

Plastic taxes remained largely unchanged in terms of scope and intensity. Italy postponed the implementation of both the Sugar Tax (until July 2025) and the Plastic Tax (until July 2026) for the fourth consecutive year. South Africa increased its plastic bag levy, while the United Kingdom announced the future introduction of a mass balance approach that allows businesses to demonstrate recycled content in packaging containing chemically recycled plastic for the purposes of the Plastic Packaging Tax.

Table 3.12. Changes to other environmentally related taxes

	Rate decrease/Base narrowing	Rate increase/Base broadening
Plastic tax		ZAF
Tourism tax		GRC, ISL, TCA
Other tax		LVA

Source: Tax Policy Reform questionnaire.

3.6. Taxes on property

There was a notable reduction in reforms raising taxes on property in 2024. Whereas in 2023 reforms were relatively balanced between tax cuts and tax increases, 2024 saw a trend towards rate decreases and base narrowing measures. Reductions in property taxes were introduced for a variety of reasons, with countries aiming to reduce the tax burden on households, facilitate housing market entry, simplify their tax systems, and support investment. Where tax increases were implemented, governments mainly cited revenue-raising and equity or fairness concerns.

In continuation from previous years, property tax reforms were mainly implemented in three key areas: inheritance, estate and gift taxes, property transaction taxes, and recurrent taxes on immovable property. Against the backdrop of elevated rents and housing prices in many countries, the overwhelming majority of reforms, both permanent and temporary, focused on residential immovable property. In most cases, however, the expected revenue impact of these measures was relatively modest. Several countries also made changes to their inheritance, estate and gift taxes. Similarly to 2024, there were very few reforms to wealth taxes.

3.6.1. Property taxes remained a small share of total tax revenues in most jurisdictions

Property taxes continue to make up a relatively small share of total tax revenues in most countries but remain significantly more important in HICs than in MICs and LICs (Figure 3.7). In 2022, property taxes accounted for 5.6% of total tax revenues in HICs, compared to just 1.9% in MICs and under 1% in LICs. While property tax revenues declined slightly across all income groups relative to 2019, HICs still rely on these taxes much more heavily. This continued reliance reflects their broader administrative capacity, well-developed property markets, and the use of recurrent property taxes as a key local government revenue source. By contrast, limited tax administration infrastructure and valuation systems in many lower-income countries continue to constrain property tax yields.

There remains substantial cross-country variation in the contribution of property taxes to overall revenues. In 2022, they made up less than 1% of total tax revenue in countries such as Estonia, the Czech Republic, and Lithuania, but exceeded 10% in the United States, Canada, the United Kingdom, and Korea. Israel recorded the highest share among OECD countries at 12.3%. Most property tax revenue comes from recurrent taxes on immovable property – typically levied at the subnational level – while transaction taxes, inheritance and gift taxes, and net wealth taxes also contribute.

Figure 3.7. Property tax revenues as a share of total tax revenues

Property tax revenues as a percentage of total tax revenues

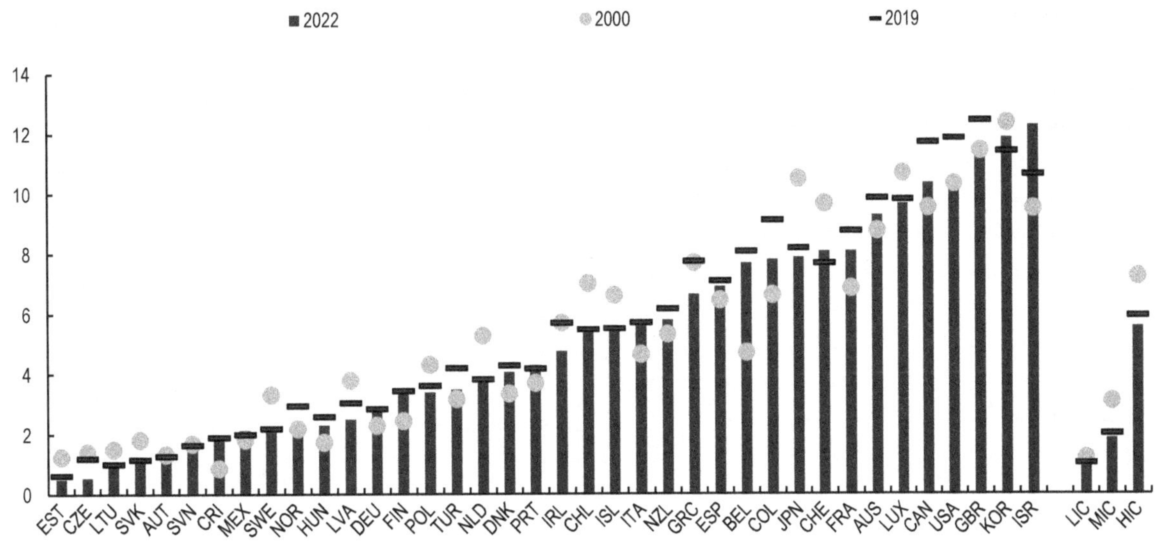

Note: Property tax revenues refer to tax category 4000 under the OECD classification of taxes. Tax revenues are the sum of taxes collected by all levels of government. See Revenue Statistics Interpretative Guide for more detail. The low-(LIC), middle-(MIC), and high-income country (HIC) averages are representative of the 116 jurisdictions that provide tax revenue data to the OECD.
Source: Global Revenue Statistics Database.

StatLink https://stat.link/v1d2hm

3.6.2. Fewer countries relied on property tax increases to raise revenues compared to previous years

Ireland and the United Kingdom increased recurrent taxes on immovable property. Ireland further raised the rate of the Vacant Homes Tax from five to seven times the standard Local Property Tax rate. Meanwhile, the United Kingdom announced private schools will be removed from eligibility for charitable rate relief on non-domestic property.

Several countries implemented targeted increases to transaction taxes. Andorra introduced a new tax on foreign real estate investment, with rates ranging from 3% to 10% depending on the specific type of real estate investment. Ireland increased the stamp duty on bulk acquisition of houses (10 or more units over a one-year period) by 5 percentage points to 15%. Additionally, Ireland introduced a new 6% stamp duty rate on residential property with a value exceeding EUR 1.5 million. Similarly, Namibia introduced a new top bracket with a 12% rate for transfers of properties worth more than NAD 12 million. Additionally, Namibia adjusted the thresholds of the transfer duty on residential properties for the general increase in property prices. In Canada, British Columbia introduced a new tax on proceeds from the sale of residential real estate held for less than two years at a maximum rate of 20% on properties sold within a year of purchase. The Canadian province of Alberta announced the replacement of its land title and mortgage registration charges with a higher new Land Titles Registration Levy for property transfers and mortgage registrations. Hungary abolished the exemption for hybrid cars from transfer duty.

The United Kingdom announced a series of significant inheritance tax base broadening measures. Taking effect in 2026, the current 100% relief on qualifying business and agricultural assets will be limited to GBP 1 million of combined assets. A new 50% relief rate applies above this threshold as well as for all shares not listed on recognised stock exchanges. Additionally, from 2027, most unused pension funds and death benefits will be included in a person's estate for inheritance tax purposes.

3.6.3. Countries continued to implement property tax cuts aiming to support investment and lower the tax burden on households

Several jurisdictions decreased recurrent taxes on immovable property to reduce the tax burden on households and certain businesses. Greece doubled the tax credit on property taxes for individuals who insure their residential properties up to a value of EUR 500 0000 against earthquakes, fires, and floods to 20%. Barbados introduced a 20% rebate on the assessed land tax for residential properties that suffer from perennial flooding due to rainfall. Macau (China) implemented a MOP 3 500 property tax deduction for residents, while also decreasing the rate for rental property by 2 percentage points to 8%. To account for the increase in market values, Singapore raised the annual value brackets of the owner-occupier residential property tax rates. Poland reduced property taxes for garages and parking spaces in residential buildings by applying the same rate as for residential buildings (previously the non-residential rate applied). The United Kingdom announced a temporary 40% relief on business rates for the retail, hospitality, and leisure sectors up to a GBP 110 000 cap. Additionally, while the business rate liability for standard non-residential property was adjusted for inflation, the business rate liability for small businesses was frozen until 2026.

Multiple provinces of Canada announced changes to recurrent taxes on immovable property. Manitoba announced the Education Property Tax Credit and School Tax Rebate will be replaced by a Homeowners Affordability Tax Credit of up to CAD 1 500, which effectively eliminates education property taxes for homes valued at approximately CAD 285 000 or less. Alberta, meanwhile, announced a freeze on education property tax rates for residential (and farmland) as well as non-residential property. British Columbia raised the maximum threshold of its homeowner grant, which can reduce the amount of property taxes paid each year on one's principal residence. Lastly, Prince Edward Island announced an increase in the maximum income threshold for the Seniors Property Tax Deferral Program.

Several jurisdictions introduced cuts to transaction taxes on immovable property used as a primary residence. Portugal introduced tax exemptions for taxpayers under 36 years of age on purchases of immovable properties in urban areas exclusively destined for use as permanent residence up to a certain taxable value. Luxembourg implemented a temporary increase of the tax credit from EUR 30 000 to EUR 40 000 while also temporarily reducing the taxable base by half for individuals buying a home for own use. In Canada, British Columbia announced expansions of its first-time home buyers' exemption and newly built home exemption via additional partial exemptions on properties whose above market value exceeds the existing full exemption thresholds. New qualifying purpose-built rental buildings will also be exempted from the general property transfer tax.

More broadly, jurisdictions lowered transaction taxes to support investment. Argentina repealed the real estate transaction tax for individuals. The Netherlands reduced the base rate of its real estate transaction tax of 10.4% to 8%, which will come into effect in 2026. Saint Lucia introduced a stamp duty exemption for the first XCD 400 000 on mortgage for the construction of a new residential home or repairs and renovation of an existing home. As part of its revised real estate transaction tax framework aimed at increasing regulatory clarity, Saudi Arabia introduced a range of exceptions and exemptions, providing certain benefits to companies and investment funds in particular. Indonesia introduced a range of fiscal incentives to aid the development of its Nusantara Capital City, including reduced taxation on the transfer of rights of land and real estate. Sweden announced the abolishment of the stamp duty on ship mortgages.

Two countries (Denmark and Germany) made cuts to their gift, estate, and inheritance taxes. Denmark announced a decrease in the inheritance and gift tax rates on family-owned businesses passed on to close family members by 5 percentage points to 10%. Additionally, Denmark announced the introduction of a statutory right to schematic valuation of businesses while the capital gains upon transfer of a real estate business can be deferred if certain conditions are met. Germany extended the 10% tax exemption of the value of real property rented for residential purposes to properties located in third countries with sufficient exchange of information. Germany also inflation-adjusted the amount of its fixed allowance to cover the cost of the deceased's funeral as well as the cost of settling and distributing the inheritance.

Argentina implemented changes to its wealth tax. It introduced a temporary and voluntary advanced payments regime under which taxpayers can make one advance payment to avoid further tax return filing and tax payment obligations until the fiscal year 2027. Those joining the regime benefit from lower fixed tax rates of 0.45% for unreported assets and 0.50% for those previously included in Argentina's disclosure regime. Any increases in net worth occurring during the period covered by the regime also do not lead to additional tax liabilities. Additionally, Argentina upward-adjusted the thresholds of the wealth tax.

Table 3.13. Changes to property taxes

	Base broadening/Rate increase		Base narrowing/Rate decrease	
	2023	2024 or later	2023	2024 or later
Estate duties, inheritance, and gift taxes	NLD[3]	GBR[3]	DNK[3], PRT, ANG, SAU	DEU, DNK[3],
Transaction taxes on movable and immovable property	AUS, BEL, BHS, CAN[3] MLT, FIN, NLD, PRT[4], SGP	AND, CAN[5], HUN, IRL	CAN[3], FIN, GRC, IND, KOR[4]	ARG, CAN[1,5], IDN, LUX, NLD, PRT, SAU, SWE
Recurrent taxes on immovable property	AUS, BHS, CAN[5], CZE, IRL, NLD, ROU, SYC	CAN[5], GBR, IRL	AIA, CAN[5], DNK, GBR[1], GRC, MAC, SWE, UKR	BRB, CAN[5], GBR, GRC, LCA, MAC, POL, SGP
Recurrent taxes on (net) wealth	COL[2,4], NOR[4]			ARG

Note: 1 denotes a temporary tax measure, 2 denotes a new tax, 3 denotes reform announcement, 4 denotes reforms introduced in 2023, but covered in last year's TPR edition, 5 denotes a reform made at sub-central level.
Source: OECD Annual Tax Policy Reform Questionnaire

References

European Commission (2025), *Reducing emissions from the shipping sector*, https://climate.ec.europa.eu/eu-action/transport/reducing-emissions-shipping-sector_en. [16]

Expert Group for Green Tax Reform (2022), *Green Tax Reform - Final Report*, https://skm.dk/media/tngh1b4r/green-tax-reform-final-report.pdf. [14]

IMO (2023), *IMO Strategy on Reducing GHG Emissions from Ships*, https://www.imo.org/en/OurWork/Environment/Pages/2023-IMO-Strategy-on-Reduction-of-GHG-Emissions-from-Ships.aspx. [15]

OECD (2025), "Tax Challenges Arising from the Digitalisation of the Economy – Administrative Guidance on the Global Anti-Base Erosion Model Rules (Pillar Two), Central Record of Legislation with Transitional Qualified Status", *OECD/G20 Inclusive Framework on BEPS*, https://www.oecd.org/content/dam/oecd/en/topics/policy-sub-issues/global-minimum-tax/administrative-guidance-globe-rules-pillar-two-central-record-legislation-transitional-qualified-status.pdf. [8]

OECD (2024), *Consumption Tax Trends 2024: VAT/GST and Excise, Core Design Features and Trends*, OECD Publishing, Paris, https://doi.org/10.1787/dcd4dd36-en. [9]

OECD (2024), *Corporate Tax Statistics 2024*, OECD Publishing, Paris, https://doi.org/10.1787/9c27d6e8-en. [1]

OECD (2024), *Prevention of Tax Treaty Abuse – Sixth Peer Review Report on Treaty Shopping: Inclusive Framework on BEPS: Action 6*, OECD/G20 Base Erosion and Profit Shifting Project, OECD Publishing, Paris, https://doi.org/10.1787/36cebf8e-en. [5]

OECD (2024), *Revenue Statistics 2024: Health Taxes in OECD Countries*, OECD Publishing, Paris, https://doi.org/10.1787/c87a3da5-en. [12]

OECD (2024), *Tax Policy Reforms 2024: OECD and Selected Partner Economies*, OECD Publishing, Paris, https://doi.org/10.1787/c3686f5e-en. [7]

OECD (2024), *Tobacco Taxation in Latin America and the Caribbean: A Call for Tobacco Tax Reform*, OECD Publishing, Paris, https://doi.org/10.1787/080cd662-en. [11]

OECD (2023), *BEPS Action 14 on More Effective Dispute Resolution Mechanisms – Peer Review Documents*, http://www.oecd.org/tax/beps/beps-action-14-on-more-effective-dispute-resolution-peer-reviewdocuments.pdf. [6]

OECD (2023), *Corporate Tax Statistics 2023*, OECD Publishing, Paris, https://doi.org/10.1787/f1f07219-en. [2]

OECD (2023), "Income-based tax relief for R&D and innovation: An integrated view", *OECD Science, Technology and Industry Policy Papers*, No. 161, OECD Publishing, Paris, https://doi.org/10.1787/2db44e8b-en. [3]

OECD (2023), *OECD/G20 Inclusive Framework on BEPS: Progress Report September 2022-September 2023*, OECD Publishing, Paris, https://doi.org/10.1787/a9ee1aef-en. [4]

OECD (2022), *Pricing Greenhouse Gas Emissions: Turning Climate Targets into Climate Action*, OECD Series on Carbon Pricing and Energy Taxation, OECD Publishing, Paris, https://doi.org/10.1787/e9778969-en. [13]

OECD (2017), *International VAT/GST Guidelines*, OECD Publishing, Paris, https://doi.org/10.1787/9789264271401-en. [10]

Notes

[1] The countries covered in this report are: Albania, Andorra, Angola, Anguilla, Argentina, Armenia, Australia, Austria, Azerbaijan, Barbados, Belgium, Belize, Bosnia and Herzegovina, Brazil, British Virgin Islands, Brunei Darussalam, Bulgaria, Canada, Cayman Islands, Chile, Colombia, Democratic Republic of Congo, Cook Islands, Costa Rica, Croatia, Curaçao, Czechia, Denmark, Dominican Republic, Estonia, Finland, France, Georgia, Germany, Greece, Greenland, Guernsey, Honduras, Hungary, Iceland, Indonesia, Ireland, Isle of Man, Israel, Italy, Japan, Kenya, Korea, Latvia, Lithuania, Luxembourg, Macau

(China), Malta, Mauritius, Mexico, Montenegro, Montserrat, Namibia, Netherlands, New Zealand, Nigeria, North Macedonia, Norway, Papua New Guinea, Peru, Poland, Portugal, Romania, Saint Lucia, Saudi Arabia, Serbia, Singapore, Slovak Republic, Slovenia, South Africa, Spain, Sweden, Switzerland, Trinidad and Tobago, Türkiye, Turks and Caicos Islands, Ukraine, United Arab Emirates, United Kingdom, United States, and Uruguay.

[2] Registered under the Small Business Development Act, Cap. 318C.

[3] Since 2018, Latvia has adopted a distribution system whereby corporate tax is levied only on profit distributions or deemed distributions. Undistributed profits are therefore tax exempt. Deemed distributions include non-business expenses, bad debts, excess interests, etc.

[4] In principle, the application of the zero-rated VAT rate to supplies, intra-community acquisitions, imports, and installations of photovoltaic modules started January 2024 and ended in March 2025. However, the zero-rated VAT rate applies until December 2025, if the underlying contracts for supplies, intra-community acquisitions, imports, and installations were concluded before March 7, 2025.